TWENTIETH-CENTURY MUSIC IDIOMS

TWENTIETH-CENTURY

G. Welton Marquis *professor and head, department of music, the university of british columbia*

MUSIC IDIOMS

PRENTICE-HALL, INC., ENGLEWOOD CLIFFS, NEW JERSEY

Printed in the United States of America 93491-C

Second printing........December, 1964

PRENTICE-HALL INTERNATIONAL, INC., London
PRENTICE-HALL OF AUSTRALIA, PTY., LTD., Sydney
PRENTICE-HALL OF CANADA, LTD., Toronto
PRENTICE-HALL OF INDIA (PRIVATE) LTD., New Delhi
PRENTICE-HALL OF JAPAN, INC., Tokyo
PRENTICE-HALL DE MEXICO, S.A., Mexico City

for Greta

Preface

Perhaps the most difficult and puzzling aspect of study confronting the Twentieth-Century student of counterpoint and harmony is the "escape" from tonal or traditional idioms to atonal or contemporary idioms. The apparent gap between the Nineteenth and the Twentieth Centuries is bridged with extreme difficulty if it is bridged at all. How does one leave the familiar order of well-regulated tonics, dominants, and key relationships without plunging into the ostensible chaos of unknowns? How does one leave the tidy world of rules and travel in a world of apparent lawlessness?

Unfortunately—tragically, one must say—there is seldom any choice for the student of music or the intellectually curious layman but to plunge headfirst into this shadowy world with little hope ever of gaining a true understanding of it. A relative few learn some of the academic aspects of Schoenberg's techniques without understanding their flexibilities and expansions. Some students may also imitate such composers as Bartók, Hindemith, Stravinsky, or Webern without fathoming their true styles. The majority, if they progress so far, flounder in a harmonic and contrapuntal sea in which Nineteenth- and Twentieth-Century tides ebb and flow. Very few are able to compose without concocting an eclectic mixture of old and pseudo-new. All too few are able to conduct, perform, or listen to the various Twentieth-Century styles with true understanding.

Perhaps the most tragic element of all is the fact that disturbing numbers of schools of music and conservatories continue to insist that only composition students need develop some knowledge of Twentieth-Century practices. Pianists, singers, violinists, public school teachers, and musicologists are still led up to the middle of the Nineteenth Century in music theory and turned out with no further knowledge, except that which may be obtained at the end of a general music history course. And most of these musicians will live in the twenty-*first* century!

Fortunately, a growing number of schools realize that *all* music students must gain an understanding of contemporary idioms and that there is no mystery inherent within these idioms that cannot be solved by logical study. The Twentieth Century, in spite of apparent lack of good sense and logic, is guided by its own rules, whether we refer to Schoenberg, Webern, Bartók, or John Cage, and the student can be led forward with comparative ease to this understanding.

One of the greatest hurdles facing the student and the teacher has been the sincere but misguided belief that one cannot "teach" Twentieth-Century counterpoint and harmony, because no rules have been formulated. Many teachers have felt that the only way to lead the student into the present century is to show him the styles used by contemporary composers and allow the student to find his own road to the future. A few extraordinary teachers have been able to give their students a true understanding of modern idioms by sheer intuition, but most of us possess no such miraculous powers.

It is obvious that the study of contemporary scores is of great importance, but the uninitiated student with Bartók's *Fourth String Quartet* in his hands may remain uninitiated. One might just as well begin the first-year study of traditional harmony with an analysis of Wagner's *Tristan und Isolde*. If the student learns to "write in the composer's style" through the study of scores alone, he has learned little except for some contrapuntal and harmonic patterns which mean little out of context.

The truth is, however, that theoretical rules have been formulated during the last fifty or sixty years, and if they seem nebulous at times, one must bear in mind that Beethoven did not compose with theory book in hand. It is particularly heartening to see a trickle of contemporary theory books appearing on the market at last—books which list harmonic, contrapuntal, and formal rules that can guide the inquiring student as surely as the traditional rules led him to an understanding of previous centuries.

Rules, after all, are formulated by theorists who conduct musical post-mortems on significant compositions of the past, and these rules serve simply as useful guides which may be disregarded entirely or in part as experience gains the upper hand. Experience, in the form of good sense and logic coupled with imagination, then formulates new rules for later theorists to note and codify.

The rules that are encountered in this book have guided the important composers of the first half of the Twentieth Century, even though such composers may have followed these dictums unconsciously—the instinct of great creative artists. An understanding of these rules will aid the young composer to enter the century in which he *must* live. Such an understanding will aid the performer to play or sing Twentieth-Century music with increased sensitivity. Curious non-professional musicians and others in present-day audiences who have some background in traditional theory will be able to expand their own horizons through the study of these rules and practices. It goes without saying that the conductor with no understanding of Twentieth-Century theory will never enter this century—nor should he.

I am exceedingly grateful to Professors Cortland Hultberg and Elliot Weisgarber of the Department of Music, the University of British Columbia, for their careful readings of the manuscript. Their suggestions were invaluable and if they were not heeded in toto, it is only because I am stubborn, and perhaps not always wise.

Sincere thanks are also due to Dr. George K. Evans, Mr. Lorne Forstner, Mr. Eric Campbell, Mrs. Raeia Maes, and others of Prentice-Hall, Inc. for their aid and encouragement in times of stress and strain.

G. WELTON MARQUIS

Contents

Introduction

A book on traditional harmony or counterpoint does not teach us to write in the style of any one composer, regardless of stylistic examples sprinkled throughout the book. We may *try* to imitate Palestrina or Bach or Schumann, but our efforts would only prove the impossibility of the task. Our "Palestrina" would be indistinguishable from Lassus or Victoria, our "Bach" from Handel, and "Schumann" from Liszt or Chopin in terms of counterpoint or harmony.

The best that we can claim for such books is that we learn general principles of theory pertaining to a given idiom and period and that these principles may enable us to perform, conduct and listen to this music with understanding. Some of us will then continue to study scores in an effort to gain a more detailed knowledge of the music of all ages.

It is this writer's fervent hope that the present book will help accomplish these things in terms of Twentieth-Century music. It does not pretend or wish to teach the inquiring person to write in the style of any one Twentieth-Century composer. It should, however, help the reader to understand the styles of all Twentieth-Century composers.

This book is directed toward five general categories of readers: the composer beginning to work in contemporary styles; the instrumental performer and singer; the conductor; the music teacher in public schools, universities, conservatories, or private studios; and the intelligent listener or amateur musician who may or may not be connected with any of the four preceding categories.

The writer assumes that all of these have had some basic instruction in tonal theory, but he does not share the belief of some who contend that many years of devout labor studying Palestrina, Fux, and traditional harmony must precede the study of modern practices. It is obvious to all that a musician should be well-grounded in the theory of all musical eras, including those which antedate Palestrina, but if this musician never reaches the Twentieth Century, he will be in the unenviable position of the physicist who finally gains an understanding of Newton, a respectable accomplishment, but a trifle out of date in the eyes of his colleagues.

For various reasons, many of the musical examples in this book have been prepared by the writer, who makes no pretense of seeking canonization as a composer. However, ready-made examples are often more effective in illustrating procedures to be followed in early stages of learning. Nevertheless, many examples from significant Twentieth-Century compositions are included for the sake of further clarification. The number of these compositions has been kept to a minimum so that all of the music may be readily available in class. It should be noted that all parts for transposing instruments in the examples sound as written.

This book begins by asking us to "forget" our knowledge of traditional harmony. It asks us not to outline triads in melodic lines and to avoid such familiar forms harmonically. It asks us to avoid the "modes," which have been used by some composers during this century. It asks these things only as a temporary expedient, because it is this writer's firm conviction that we must avoid Nineteenth-Century forms if we are to understand all of the music written in the Twentieth Century.

The writer does not condemn Hindemith's triads, Vaughan-Williams' modal harmonies or the raised and lowered thirds which veil William Schuman's triads. In fact, these, or similar forms, will be discussed in a later chapter, but an examination of such techniques does little to aid the beginning student to understand Schoenberg's *Pierrot Lunaire* or Webern's *String Quartet*, Op. 28.

We are asked to consider the scale as being composed of twelve equally important tones unrelated to traditional key centers. Instrumental or vocal sonorities are to be considered at all times, so that the learning will have practical implications. It is suggested strongly that *all* exercises be written for available instrumental and/or vocal ensembles and performed in class instead of being written for some undesignated instruments and perhaps hammered out on the piano, or, worse still, never played at all, but just graded by a teacher at a desk.

This book is intended to be the basis of instruction in the third or fourth year of study in a department or school of music, although there is sufficient material in it to be used during two academic years. It is to be hoped that students in all musical areas will have an opportunity to study its materials, because all who pretend to be musicians in the Twentieth Century should know this century well.

If this book does not try to answer all Twentieth-Century theoretical questions, the writer is still hopeful that it will stimulate the study of contemporary idioms. It is a rather unconventional book, a fact that does not embarrass the writer in the least. If it has merits, it will accomplish only what a book such as this should accomplish: to serve as a guide for intelligent and flexible teaching and for intellectually curious men and women who want to live musically in their own century.

TWENTIETH-CENTURY MUSIC IDIOMS

1 / *the melodic line*

THE PROBLEM OF UNDERSTANDING One of the main keys to the understanding of the non-tonal music of the Twentieth Century is the conception of the melodic line as it has changed during the last fifty or sixty years—indeed, as it has changed throughout the ages. If we consider modern melody unmusical and corrupted, we must bear in mind that we may be expressing a historical distaste for the new—and that history has always proven us wrong.

We need not elaborate here on Plato's sorrow or on the sorrow of similar figures throughout history who have longed for "the good old days" when musical composition (or painting, sculpture, architecture, literature or child-rearing) was in secure and honest hands. The "good old days" never returned in music because of such "radical" composers as Philippe de Vitry, Guillaume de Machaut, Dufay, Willaert, Gesualdo, Monteverdi, Johann Stamitz, Beethoven, Berlioz, Wagner, Debussy—great composers whose names have been italicized by history.

The Twentieth Century has had its quota of pioneers whose music appeared to transcend the bounds of esthetic decency when it was first performed. Yet much of this music is now accepted as conventional or even old-fashioned by many intelligent listeners while other "radicals" continue to forge ahead, confounding those who have just begun to accept the music of Arnold Schoenberg.

1

Most of us, however—teachers, students, performers, conductors, and audiences—are still musical children of the Eighteenth and Nineteenth Centuries by instinct, training, and exposure. Conditioned as we are to the music of Haydn, Beethoven, Schubert, Tchaikovsky, and their contemporaries, we find it difficult to understand a melodic line that appears to disobey all the "rules" as we know them.

For example, we may see or hear a melodic line such as the following and ridicule its leaps and total lack of harmonic outline.

1 Webern *Variations for Orchestra,* Op. 30 (pp. 23–24)
Reprinted by permission of Universal Edition A. G., Vienna and Associated Music Publishers, Inc., New York.

But we can turn back one hundred years to Beethoven's *Great Fugue* and see that this composer was also exploring similar esthetic realms.

Allegro

2 Beethoven *Great Fugue*, Op. 133

Or we may go back over two hundred years and find the human voice challenged in this manner.

ar___ ci___ sal___ ta___ te, tut - to

3 Pergolesi *Il maestro di musica* (Collaggiani's aria)

Actually, almost all great composers throughout the ages have explored the use of contrasts between high and low points in a melodic line in order to achieve particular emotional effects. This can be accomplished through flowing lines which soar to the upper range of an

3

instrument or voice and plummet to a lower register. Or, as in Beethoven's *Great Fugue*, the line is jagged, creating a nervous emotional tension. Many Twentieth-Century composers have merely extended this concept either by requiring more of their performers or by constructing new sounds in an electronics laboratory. But the trend has always been to increase the demands on instrumentalists and vocalists.

If we accept this historical fact that melodic lines may leap from one register to another, it may still be extremely difficult to understand or accept the line which does not suggest or outline the traditional harmony that we know so well. Nineteenth-Century composers in particular tended to follow chordal outlines with their melodies, and our ears often refuse to accept a break with this tradition.

However, the music of the past again is full of melodic lines that are harmonically ambiguous and that seem to lack a clearly defined sense of harmonic direction. It is not necessary to turn to Richard Wagner or to Hugo Wolf. Consider, for example, the following familiar melody.

4 Beethoven *Sonata in E Flat for Piano*, Op. 81a

Furthermore, we tend to forget that melodic lines, per se, are not essential to musical composition. That is, history has preserved a great mass of music which represents the composers' fascination for sonorities alone. This urge to depict musical moods through the use of kaleidoscopic harmonies, brilliant chromatic passages, and percussive chords and rhythms which exist with little or no reference to singable melodies is present in the music of most composers. Johann Sebastian Bach's toccatas, Beethoven's "Moonlight" and other sonatas, Liszt's and Chopin's pyrotechnics, and Debussy's total output all illustrate this urge.

If we are to work with present-day idioms, we must reach an understanding of the "non-harmonic"—or non-traditional-melodic line. Many of our most significant composers consciously avoid lines that suggest traditional harmonic forms in any way, although some composers are more conservative. However, the composer who attempts to graft Twentieth-Century counterpoint and harmony to a Nineteenth-Century melodic frame will create a work which may be false to both centuries.

This is not to say that the triad is obsolete. It may be obsolescent, as we will see later, and the conductor, composer, performer, or listener who construes the main stream of modern music in terms of tonic, dominant, and traditional modulations will never comprehend the constant evolution of the art.

BASIC RULES It is obvious that Mozarts and Schuberts do not learn to write melodies in schools of music or conservatories. However, the technique of composing melodic lines may be learned up to a certain point, after which "inspiration" and/or "genius" (if present) take command.

There are rules of melody writing which a few follow intuitively, but most composers need to be reminded of certain features inherent in effective composition before their own weaker intuitions operate. Although Twentieth-Century melody may differ with each composer—as it has throughout the ages—the basic rules remain the same, and these rules will differ remarkably little from those used instinctively by Franz Schubert.

Perhaps the greatest hazard confronting the person who attempts to write a non-traditional melodic line is something which the author calls "wanderitis." This is a tendency to consider an endless series of half-steps, leaps, and linear contortions as "modern." In an effort to avoid triads and other tonal formations, the beginner may wander aimlessly. (Contrary to public opinion, the sound of the family cat strolling along the keyboard can be distinguished from Bartok's *Miraculous Mandarin*.)

"Wanderitis" can be avoided melodically by using more scalewise patterns coupled with a carefully selected amount of chromaticism. If, after some time, chromaticism and jaggedness prove to be the basis of our compositional style, the choice is our prerogative, but in the beginning it is wise to follow a more conservative course.

The contemporary melody may be of any length, although in the beginning stages of learning there is no point in attempting to write extremely long lines. These may be composed later with greater ease. On the other hand, if the first melodic attempts are too short, they will serve little instructional purpose.

It should be apparent that no key signatures are necessary and that a melodic line may begin and end on any tone. We are not concerned with tonics now. Accidentals should be written solely for ease of performance, but in general, the traditional rule of sharps ascending and flats descending should be observed.

Ex. 5

Before we discuss the various aspects of melodic writing in more detail, we shall list a set of fundamental guides for this new contrapuntal and harmonic world. Most of these rules pertain to melodic writing in any era, but some are related solely to music of the Twentieth Century. All of them are guides, and later, some or all of these rules may be discarded consciously, but in the beginning, we will do well to observe them carefully and keep them firmly in mind.

1) *Try to avoid outlining traditional chords in the melodic line.*

Ex. 6

By traditional chords we mean, in particular, any type of triad or seventh chord consisting of a major triad and a minor seventh. If other traditional forms can be avoided at this time, so much the better. It is obvious, of course, that many significant composers of this century do not observe this rule, but if we can avoid such melodic outlines now, we will understand *all* contemporary idioms more easily.

For example, Paul Hindemith may outline triads as follows.

Vlns. I

(𝅗𝅥. = 50~54)

7 Hindemith *The Four Temperaments* (pp. 12–13)

Reprinted by permission of B. Schott's Soehne, Mainz, Schott & Co., Ltd., London and Associated Music Publishers, Inc. New York.

And yet he tends to avoid them in other passages.

Vlns. I

(𝅘𝅥 = about 100)

8 Hindemith *The Four Temperaments* (p. 1)

Reprinted by permission of B. Schott's Soehne, Mainz, Schott & Co., Ltd., London and Associated Music Publishers, Inc., New York.

Anton Webern may avoid them almost entirely.

9 Webern *Five Pieces for String Quartet*, Op. 5 (p. 4)
Reprinted by permission of Universal Edition A. G., Vienna and Associated Music Publishers, Inc., New York.

Furthermore, such traditional chords are foreign to most twelve-tone music, and even though exceptions may be found, the following line is typical.

10 Schoenberg *Fourth String Quartet* (p. 37)
Copyright, 1939, by G. Schirmer, Inc. Reprinted by permission.

2) *Try to avoid skipping over the barlines during the initial stages of learning.*

Ex. 11.

The reason for this rule is that a leap of more than a third to the first note of a measure may introduce a jarring effect which is not intended by the beginning composer. For the same reason, a leap in any direction from a weak to a strong beat should be avoided unless the resulting effect is desired consciously. When we discuss two-part writing in the next chapter, however, we will find that such a leap in one voice may be counterbalanced by half- or whole-step movement in the other voice.

The following passage is a good example of effective smooth writing which tends to incorporate Rule 2.

12 Weisgarber *Divertimento* (p. 18)
Reprinted by permission of Camara Music Publishers, New York.

However, note in the next example how Bartók creates an entirely different effect through the use of leaps from weak to strong beats.

13 Bartók *Violin Concerto* (p. 13)
Copyright 1946 by Hawkes & Son (London) Ltd. Reprinted by permission of Boosey & Hawkes Inc.

Obviously, the impact of such leaps varies with the type(s) of instrument employed, dynamic markings, register, rhythmic pattern, tempo, and other considerations, since these elements cannot be separated from composition.

3) *Try to avoid more than one leap in the same direction, and after any skip of more than a third, attempt to bring the line back by a half or whole step.*

Ex 14

There are two basic reasons for this rule. Students of traditional counterpoint realize that two or more leaps in the same direction tend to destroy a melody's equilibrium by extending the line too rapidly. This may also be the case in contemporary writing. Furthermore, two skips in the same direction are likely to outline a traditional chord, which we should avoid at this time.

Like any rule, this one is flexible in the hands of an experienced composer. Nevertheless, note how Roger Sessions tends to follow it in a line that includes wide leaps.

15 *Sessions Quintet (p. 8)*
Reprinted by permission of Edward B. Marks Music Corporation, New York.

4) *Avoid melodic jaggedness during the first stages of learning.*

Ex. 16

In Rules 2 and 3 above we have cautioned against the use of two leaps in the same direction and wide skips from weak to strong beats. However, even if we employ some leaps, a continuous pattern of jaggedness should be avoided at this time, because such lines are too difficult for the inexperienced student to handle melodically or contrapuntally. We should try to write in a more scalewise manner using occasional skips and leaps for variety and interest.

5) *Make the melody lead to some climactic goal; do not let it wander aimlessly by inserting arbitrary accidentals.*

Ex. 17

This rule will be discussed in detail later in this chapter when we start the actual construction of contemporary melodic lines. Obviously, this rule involves not only the choice of melodic intervals but the planning of melodic curves, rhythmic patterns, meter, and other facets of composition.

6) Avoid repeating a note on strong beats of nearby measures.

Ex. 18

In modern or traditional writing, one of the traps that ensnares the beginning composer is the unconscious repetition of tones on the first or strong beats of adjacent measures. This, of course, introduces a monotony which is seldom intended. There are times, naturally, when a composer wishes to emphasize a certain tone by accented repetition, as in the following theme.

19 Hindemith *Mathis der Maler* (p. 13)

Reprinted by permission of B. Schott's Soehne, Mainz, Schott & Co., Ltd., London and Associated Music Publishers, Inc., New York.

But the inexperienced composer should handle such tonal repetitions with special care.

7) *Avoid using the same note too frequently in a short melody.*

Ex. 20

This rule is, perhaps, even more important to the beginning composer, because it can be broken so easily while the reason for the resulting dullness is not always apparent upon a first examination of the music.

8) *Avoid two or more equal high or low points in a short melodic line.*

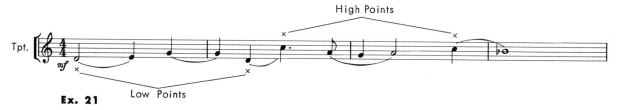

Ex. 21

17

As we shall see when we examine the subject of melodic curves (p. 24), each short melody normally contains a single climax, which is usually reached in the highest tone. For obvious reasons this climax is dulled if the same high tone or high point is repeated within the framework of a relatively short line. Although equal low points may not lessen the impact of a climax, their presence tends to introduce unintended monotony into a melody. In general, equal low points should be avoided.

In the following example, Béla Bartók uses a C for both the low and high points during the first seven measures and makes special emphasis of these tones. But the true low and high points appear in measures eight and nine, thus bringing the line to a final climax.

22 Bartók *Violin Concerto* (pp. 19–20)

9) *Avoid using the same rhythmic pattern in consecutive or nearby measures.*

(a) Avoid

Moderato

Vln.

(b) Preferable

Moderato

Vln.

Ex. 23

The problem of rhythm will also be discussed later in some detail (p. 29), but the basic rule above is broken unconsciously by every beginning composer. However, in trying to avoid this snare, we should not make the mistake of forsaking simplicity and thereby confusing artificial complexities with art.

19

10) *Avoid shifting meters during the early stages of learning and strive to "disguise" the barlines by occasional ties and through the use of displaced accents.*

Ex. 24

The excessive use of meter changes often creates "eye music" which gives the appearance of mature writing, but which would be more effective from both the performer's and listener's standpoint if fewer meter changes—if any—were used.

In the hands of an experienced composer, meter shifts can be most effective, but even he must be careful not to commit compositional fraud. Furthermore, if the beginning composer entertains the notion that such writing was invented in this century, he should examine the many late fourteenth-century compositions which include many meter changes and polyrhythms as well.

11) *Avoid symmetrical phrases and periods.*

Ex. 25

This is no hard and fast rule, but we should try to avoid phrases that answer each other symmetrically. Such a style is foreign to the atonal concept of writing, which tends to avoid such obvious symmetry. However, we should also bear in mind that an interesting eight-measure melodic line is preferable to one forced unnaturally into seven or nine measures.

Notice how Prokofieff has avoided traditional symmetry by shifting the rhythmic pattern in the first measures of the following melody.

26 Prokofieff *Violin Concerto No. 2* (pp. 3–4)

Examine the following melody by Alban Berg and note how an eight-measure phrase is made effective through the use of rhythmic shifts in the last two measures.

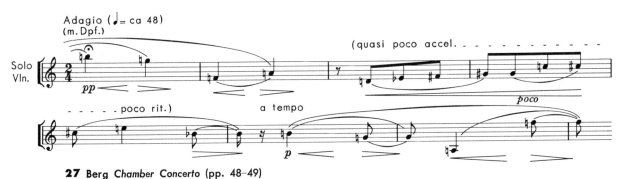

27 Berg *Chamber Concerto* (pp. 48–49)

Reprinted by permission of Universal Edition A. G., Vienna and Associated Music Publishers, Inc., New York.

12) *Attempt to keep the note values relatively large and the tempos reasonably slow during the first stages of learning.*

In other words, "Be clear, and not so clever," as the Greek dramatist, Aristophanes, wrote. It is frequently stated—with less humor than may be expected—that any competent "academic composer" can create respectable fast movements where lack of inspiration may be concealed by knowledge of theory and frenetic energy. The supreme test lies in the slow movements where everything is open to critical ears upon a first hearing. Although we cannot draw a black line between "large" and "small" note values, we might avoid notes smaller than the eighth at first, moving gradually into more complex textures and faster tempos.

13) **Write all exercises for some definite instrument or vocal classification, and have all work performed in class.**

This rule cannot be emphasized too strongly. Unless we *hear* our mistakes and improvements, we will never understand true musical creation but gain merely a "paper" understanding of theory. An exercise graded in red pencil at the teacher's desk and never heard is wasted for the most part.

Furthermore, as we have seen, composition and a knowledge of instrumental and vocal sonorities are inseparable. Each instrument possesses an individual tone color, as do the various registers—or strings—of an instrument or human voice. A dissonant passage may sound harsh on the piano but mild if performed by strings or a flute. An ascending leap played on the A-string of a violin will assume a different character if it is played on a viola's A-string.

Thus, exercises written for an orchestral instrument but played on a piano will teach us little. And as these varying characteristics cannot be explained accurately in terms of "dark," "bright," "nasal," or other adjectives, the only way for us to learn instrumental colors is to write for these instruments and to hear the results.

MELODIC CURVES An effective melodic line must carry our ears to some goal, which must be reached in a manner convincing to our ears. Like the speech of a trained speaker, a melodic line should contain both high and low tones—inflections—which are part of a general curve or series of curves. All western melodies from Gregorian chant to the Twentieth Century are based on some type of curve.

The type of melodic curve we use depends upon where we want our climax or climaxes, great and small. It depends also on the mood we wish to achieve. In the slow movement of his *Pathetique* Sonata, Beethoven uses a series of dips and rises, the high point appearing shortly before the middle of the initial melody. Such a curve imbues the line with a feeling of calm quietude with a slight tension in the middle.

Adagio cantabile

28 Beethoven *Sonata for Piano*, Op. 13

Paul Hindemith in the Twentieth Century employs a similar curve.

29 Hindemith *First Piano Sonata* (p. 1)

The high point frequently comes at the beginning of the melody.

30 Bartók *First String Quartet* (p. 9)

A commonly used curve has the climax at the end.

31 Berg *Chamber Concerto* (p. 16)

Many times the high point will be preceded by one or more dips in the melodic line.

32 Prokofieff *Violin Concerto No. 2* (pp. 43–44)

However, while the general outline of the various curves can be plotted on paper, it is the subtle dips and the carefully planned skips and leaps that help to make melodic lines effective. Note how the following line almost immediately reaches the high point, which is then followed by a series of dips and crests.

33 Webern *Five Pieces for String Quartet*, Op. 5 (pp. 2–3)
Reprinted by permission of Universal Edition A. G., Vienna and Associated Music Publishers, Inc., New York.

The melodic curve, then, is of great importance and must be considered with care. And it is not wrong to suggest that the whole mood of a musical section may be expressed in the type of curve used. We know, for example, that tension is normally inherent within an ascending line, whereas a descending line suggests relaxation. Thus, if a melody contains a series of ascending curves which finally culminates in a high point, tension may be maintained throughout the line. But if the high point exists at the beginning of the melody and is followed by a series of descending curves, the opposite effect may be achieved. And if the melodic curve is slight, a static mood may be produced.

This, of course, must be considered in connection with other compositional elements, since the choice of dynamics, rhythm, and instruments may be of equal importance in establishing a certain mood. Also, the type of melodic intervals used is of importance, since small intervals, such as half-steps, may increase the tension in a descending passage whereas larger intervals may produce the opposite effect in a descending line.

(a) Moderato

28

(b) Moderato

Vln.

Ex. 34

RHYTHMIC PROCEDURES Of equal importance to the effectiveness of melodic lines are the rhythmic patterns we use. It is impossible to teach which patterns to employ, but it is quite possible—and necessary—to indicate the rhythmic pitfalls we should avoid.

We have already noted in Rule 9 above (p. 19) that repeated rhythmic patterns in nearby measures may make a composition dull. Obviously, repeated dance-like rhythms are not ruled out. However, Twentieth-Century art tends to avoid the obvious, and rhythmic repetition should be viewed with caution.

Although the reiteration of rhythmic patterns in adjacent measures should be avoided normally, there are times when such repetition is effective, as in the following example in which a meter change is emphasized.

Vlns. II

35 Hindemith *The Four Temperaments* (p. 2)

Reprinted by permission of B. Schott's Soehne, Mainz, Schott & Co., Ltd., London and Associated Music Publishers, Inc., New York.

However, if too many different types of rhythmic patterns are mixed together in a haphazard manner, coherency and balance are lost. This lack of rhythmic coherency may be illustrated as follows.

Cl.

Ex. 36

The following solution is better.

Ex. 37

One simple way of adding rhythmic interest and avoiding monotony is to use ties over the barlines. Such ties displace the natural strong beats of a measure, but if care is not taken, they may result in another monotonous repetition.

Ex. 38

The rhythm above would be more effective if it were varied as follows.

Flt.

Moderato

Ex. 39

A simple but interesting example of bar line displacement is as follows.

Vln. I

$(\text{\textonehalf} = 72)$

40 Piston *String Quartet No. 4* (p. 1)

Reprinted by permission of Associated Music Publishers, Inc., New York.

If one wishes to repeat a rhythmic pattern for its "hypnotic" effect, it may be wise to interrupt it by meter changes.

Ex. 41

When introducing shorter note values in a slow-moving melody, it is advisable to precede and follow them in such a way that the rhythmic flow is not impaired, as it is in the following example.

Ex. 42

The following rhythmic version would flow more smoothly.

Adagio

Flt.

Ex. 43

While rhythmic activity normally takes place on weak beats, it may be more interesting at times to vary this procedure.

Andante

Cl.

Ex. 44

An examination of scores will help us learn the many subtleties which may be employed, but when writing the first exercises, we should keep the rhythm reasonably simple yet interesting. It may be helpful to tap out the rhythm while writing the melody; this will often help us to avoid tiresome patterns.

CONSTRUCTING THE MELODIC LINE After studying the rules and other suggestions in this chapter, we may well ask: "What do we do now? Rules do not help us to choose the most effective notes." The answer, however, is simple: Write and continue to write. At first, melodic construction in any new style is bound to be a mechanical procedure, but constant practice is the solution.

We must remember one thing in the beginning: We are not now concerned with major or minor scales. Each of the twelve tones available to us is to be considered as important as all others. F♯, for example, is no longer subordinate to C or F♮ as it was in the traditional C scale. We will find, however, that certain tones become more important because we choose to make them so by repetition, accentuation, as high points, or by other compositional means.

The tendency to wander is the first writing hurdle, so let us forget meter, rhythm and dynamics for a moment and concentrate on the sequence of tones. The following series of notes may serve as an introductory illustration.

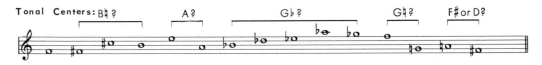

Ex. 45

First, note that the melodic curve reaches upward to a single high point shortly after the middle of the line and then descends rapidly to a note of repose.

Second, find any melodic patterns which may be useful later as development material. It is obvious that a line that proceeds mainly by half and whole steps will not serve this purpose unless rhythmic or harmonic patterns are to become the sole developmental material. But in Example 45 there are many melodic patterns which may be used in combination with rhythmic designs. For example, sections of our melodic curve may be transformed by means of rhythmic alterations and transposition.

Ex. 46

It may be noted also, that the sequence of tones in our line may be considered traditional, since the entire passage could be harmonized without great difficulty in a Nineteenth-Century manner though no major or minor triads are outlined directly. It is, in other words, a "conservative" melody that avoids obvious tonal implications. There are only a few ascending and descending leaps, all of which may be sung or played without difficulty, but which add interest to a comparatively normal line.

We have noted above in Rule 5 (p. 15) that a melodic line may wander aimlessly if accidentals are employed in an arbitrary manner. The accidentals in Example 45, however, are used to give the line a sense of direction by outlining "tonal centers" that have only a vague relationship with traditional tonal centers. We may note that the second, third, and fourth tones in Example 45 revolve, perhaps, about a B tonal center; an A center may be established for notes five and six; the next five tones seem to revolve about G♭; G♮ may be the center of the following two notes; and either D or F♯ may be the center for the last two tones. These tonal centers are intentionally vague, but they exist because of the relationship between groups of tones.

The feeling of direction is accomplished here chiefly by two methods. Half steps may lead to a tone that is foreign to the preceding tonal center, as in notes one and two, six and seven, and eleven and twelve. However, if too many half steps are employed, the melody may lose its sense of direction—"wanderitis" again.

The second way of establishing new tonal centers is by the use of leaps—particularly ascending and descending leaps of the perfect fourth or fifth. For example, the half-step movement from F to F♯ (tones one and two), followed by an ascending leap of a perfect fifth to C♯ gives our line a forceful sense of direction that might be lost if we were to skip directly from F to C♯. Although a tritone leap may be very effective if it is not overused, this rather "restless" interval has, perhaps, less melodic force than any other interval. Note in the following example the strength of the ascending perfect fourth surrounded by the more restless tritones.

Ex. 47

Now if meter, rhythm, and dynamics are added to our series of tones in Example 45 in accordance with the rules listed in this chapter, we may obtain the following melody.

Ex. 48

38

Here is a simple melodic line that incorporates an interesting rhythmic displacement of the barline and which may be considered an effective example of conservative non-traditional writing.

Let us establish one more series of tones.

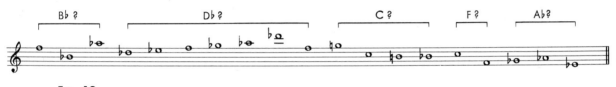

Ex. 49

Once again note the single high point, preceded and followed by a series of minor curves. Note also the use of steps and skips, which add interest to the line, and which introduce new tonal centers to give the line a sense of direction.

With meter, dynamics, and rhythm this series of tones might be used as follows.

Ex. 50

Or we might use the series in the following manner.

Ex. 51

Before writing any exercises, let us examine the following melodic excerpts in the light of what has been discussed in this chapter. Notice in Example 52 how Béla Bartók introduces tonal centers by means similar to ours. Note also the effective rhythmic patterns and the series of minor curves that finally lead to the high point in the seventh measure.

52 Bartók *First String Quartet* (p. 1)

Elliot Weisgarber employs a similar technique.

53 Weisgarber *Divertimento* (p. 7)

And Paul Hindemith writes as follows.

54 Hindemith *Mathis der Maler* (p. 6)

EXERCISES

1) Use the following series of tones and compose melodies in the treble clef for those instruments that are available in the class. Write slowly and check the rules listed in this chapter. Perform these melodies in class and discuss them analytically.

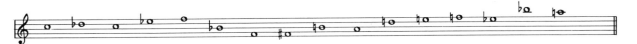

2) Construct a series of tones without meter or rhythm. Use this series to write melodies for all available treble clef instruments. Proceed as in Exercise 1.

3) Compose melodies in the bass clef, using the same resources and procedures as in the preceding exercises.

4) Using the series of tones constructed for Exercise 2, compose melodies in the alto clef for viola, if this instrument is available for performance.

5) Without constructing an unmeasured series of tones, compose more complex melodies for specific orchestral and band instruments in the various clefs. Examine each line carefully in order to avoid rhythmic and melodic dullness. Use dynamic and accent markings as well as tempo indications in all exercises. If the line is being written for a stringed instrument, bowings may also be indicated. Always discuss the melodies in class after performing them.

6) Choose various poetic texts and compose short songs without accompaniment for all voice classifications. Try to avoid symmetrical phrases by using rhythmic shifts and extensions.

7) Examine scores by Twentieth-Century composers and study their various techniques for writing melodic lines. Examine the melodic curves as well as the rhythms and meters employed, and if possible, listen with scores to phonograph recordings in class in order to study the various sounds produced by different instruments in all registers.

SCHEDULING SUGGESTIONS

Although the class time spent on this chapter will vary with the background of the students, it is recommended strongly that an examination of Chapter 2 be delayed until the materials in the present chapter have been absorbed. The techniques discussed in the remainder of this book may be grasped with comparative ease if effective melodic lines can be written.

Certainly no less than one month should be spent in melodic construction, and in most cases two months would pay surprising dividends.

2 / two-part writing

DISSONANCE AND CONSONANCE The compositional procedures used in a great deal of Twentieth-Century music are strikingly similar to those of previous centuries. Even the most extreme modern compositions may be created by extensions of these methods. Except for the type of melodic line, the only significant change is the increasing shift towards dissonance and a decided change in its treatment. But as the student of music history knows, the dissonance of one century becomes the consonance of the next; that is, dissonance is relative—its constant use tends to make it consonant to our ears.

Consider, for example, the following two-part counterpoint written toward the middle of the Fourteenth Century.

1 Guillaume de Machaut *"Je ne cuit pas qu'onques"*

The thirds and sixths marked with asterisks had been considered dissonant in previous centuries and were still treated with considerable care, even by so "progressive" a composer as Machaut. He normally considered them to be "imperfect consonances"; that is, as passing intervals between the "perfect consonances": unison, perfect fifth, and octave; or the perfect fourth between the upper voices in three- or four-part music. However, despite the quartal contrapuntal style, which emphasized perfect fourths and fifths, the accented third and sixth are common in Machaut's music, and as succeeding composers continued to use them in a more exposed manner, they were finally accepted as the main intervals in the tertian composition of the past three centuries.

In a similar manner, seconds, tritones, and sevenths were employed increasingly by composers throughout the ages to introduce tension and color into music, although they were usually handled with care. However, by Beethoven's time dissonances were no longer used solely as suspensions, passing tones, and other contrapuntal figurations. Crashing dissonances, reiterated for emphasis, were part of Beethoven's compositional vocabulary, as we see in the following example.

2 Beethoven *Sonata for Piano, Op.* 111

The continued use of such exposed dissonances led inexorably to their acceptance by later composers, who have been satisfied to treat them as stable intervals which needed no resolution. Seconds, tritones, and sevenths had completed an evolutionary phase which was longer but similar to that of the thirds and sixths. They could stand alone as entities within themselves. As such, they might be treated as consonances without need of resolution.

However, the very freedom now enjoyed by dissonance poses a difficult problem for the beginning compostion student who may consider continuous dissonance to be synonymous with modern music. Although the works of many composers might indicate that this is true, it is well to learn how to handle a combination of all kinds of intervals before moving on toward a more dissonant style.

We should not be afraid of thirds, perfect fifths, and sixths. Perfect fourths may pose an additional problem; they tend to sound dissonant in consonant passages, but consonant in dissonant writing. This may be seen in the following examples.

Ex. 3

There is obviously no rule for determining the proportion of consonances and dissonances to be used, but constant writing and listening will help to determine this in time. It might be remembered, however, that experienced ears consider certain intervals to be more or less dissonant than others. The following example illustrates the normal disposition of intervals, ranging from extreme dissonance to extreme consonance.

48

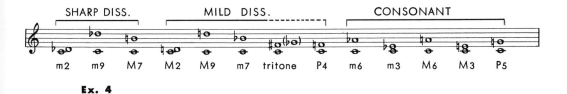

SHARP DISS.   MILD DISS.   CONSONANT

m2 m9 M7 M2 M9 m7 tritone P4 m6 m3 M6 M3 P5

Ex. 4

In other words—without entering the realms of acoustics or philosophy—we consider the minor second and the major seventh to be sharp dissonances whereas the major second and the minor seventh are viewed as soft or mild dissonances and, as we have seen, the perfect fourth is relatively dissonant in a consonant texture. Also, the tritone may appear to be a somewhat unstable interval which lends a restless quality to music. The exact order of dissonance and consonance in terms of shading is unimportant, but it *is* important to learn how to handle the varying shades of tension.

For this reason, the first rule of two-part writing may be:

1) *Mix consonance with dissonance.*

Andante

2 Cls.

Ex. 5

We will note that the music in Example 5 ranges from a feeling of relaxation to many shades of tension, causing our ears to hear it with interest. Without this mixture of consonance and dissonance, the music might become monotonous and dull.

Notice that even in twelve-tone music, consonant intervals may play an important role. Although there are no accented intervals in Example 6, the tension shifts constantly through the use of many shades of dissonance and consonance.

6 Schoenberg *Fourth String Quartet* (p. 3)

Copyright, 1939, by G. Schirmer, Inc. Reprinted by permission.

Paul Hindemith mixes consonances and dissonances as follows.

7 Hindemith *Third Piano Sonata* (4th Movement)

Reprinted by permission of B. Schott's Soehne, Mainz, Schott & Co., Ltd., London and Associated Music Publishers, Inc., New York.

In using sharp dissonances, however, it may be wise to soften the shock of their appearance by preceding and following them with milder dissonances.

Ex. 8

This procedure depends, of course, on the musical effect desired in a given passage. If the "shock" is planned consciously, then the rule has no pertinence. Sudden percussive effects may, at times, be very desirable.

2 Oboes

Ex. 9

As a corollary of the above, a second rule for two-part writing may be:

2) *Do not accent all dissonances.*

(a) Avoid

Cl.

Bsn.

(b) Preferable

Ex. 10

In the hands of the inexperienced composer, accented sharp dissonances may assume an artificial character by overuse. Later, we shall work in a more dissonant idiom, but for the moment, we should use some suspensions, passing and neighboring tones, as well as syncopated counterpoint and accented dissonances.

Ex. 11

Reexamine Example 7 and notice how Hindemith uses these techniques.

The subtle use of the various consonances and dissonances is essential, therefore, to a great deal of Twentieth-Century music. This ability can come to many of us with time; whether this ability will be accompanied by creative inspiration is another matter. Of equal importance is the fact that ability without creative genius still allows us to understand and interpret this music.

MELODIC MOVEMENT Students of tonal counterpoint know that the mastery of two-part writing is essential to effective composition and that in contrapuntal music with more than two voices, whether by Beethoven or by Hindemith, the upper and lower lines together should be interesting without the inner voice parts.

12 Beethoven *Sonata for Piano, Op. 106*

13 Hindemith *Second Piano Sonata* (3rd Movement)

Reprinted by permission of B. Schott's Soehne, Mainz, Schott & Co., Ltd., London and Associated Music Publishers, Inc., New York.

Although traditional counterpoint is concerned with obeying certain harmonic rules, contemporary counterpoint creates its own harmony through the force of its separate lines and the arrangement of its vertical intervals. In order to make the combined lines effective, we may list additional guides.

3) *In contrapuntal writing, a rest should precede the entrance of one of the lines.*

Ex. 14

Since contrapuntal music is composed of two or more voices, each of which strives for—but never attains—independence, the employment of such rests makes the entrance of a new voice more apparent to our ears.

4) *Strive for contrary motion relieved by some parallel and similar motion.*

Ex. 15

As we shall see, there are times when we may wish to employ parallel motion in the form of melodic doubling, but, as we know from our study of traditional theory, too much parallelism negates the very principle of counterpoint. This does not mean that we must avoid parallel thirds, for example, but certain parallel intervals should be avoided or used with extreme care.

Parallel octaves and unisons tend to reduce the music's texture to one thin line unless the octaves and unisons are merely the result of instrumental or vocal doubling.

Furthermore, parallel perfect fourths and fifths have been worked to death by composers who have sought to introduce a "medieval" sound into modern music. The belief that the parallel *organum* of circa 900 A.D. was characteristic of all medieval music is mistaken. It might be wise, therefore, to employ such parallel intervals with more than the usual caution.

With this in mind, Example 15 would be more effective as follows.

Ex. 16

5) *Avoid similar melodic curves in the two lines.*

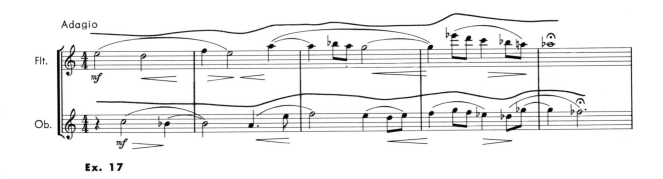

Ex. 17

The two lines should, of course, be similar in character, but to produce an effective overall musical pattern the melodic curves should be dissimilar. Because in Example 17 the high points of both lines appear simultaneously our ears perceive but one climax instead of enjoying the subtlety of two separate high points. Obviously the employment of contrary motion will help to produce dissimilar curves. For example, note the way this is accomplished by Paul Hindemith.

59

18 Hindemith *Ludus Tonalis (Fuga tertia in F)*

Reprinted by permission of B. Schott's Soehne, Mainz, Schott & Co., Ltd., London and Associated Music Publishers, Inc., New York.

Sergei Prokofieff employs dissimilar curves as follows.

19 Prokofieff *Violin Concerto No. 2 (p. 38)*

6) *Do not obscure melodic movement in one voice by conflicting movement in the other.*

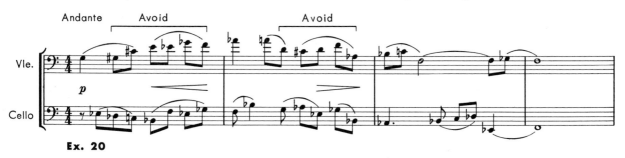

Ex. 20

Remember what has been called so aptly Bach's "cartwheel" technique of writing: one voice pauses while the other moves.

21 J. S. Bach *Two-Part Invention No. 13*

The following is an example of this technique employed in this century.

22 Carter *String Quartet* (1951) (p. 41)
Reprinted by permission of Associated Music Publishers, Inc., New York.

Obviously the "cartwheel" technique should not be allowed to become stereotyped, but the basic rule is sound. Paul Hindemith uses the following procedure.

23 Hindemith *Ludus Tonalis (Interludium 3)*
Reprinted by permission of B. Schott's Soehne, Mainz, Schott & Co., Ltd., London and Associated Music Publishers Inc.,
New York.

7) Try to keep the parts within a tenth of each other and avoid excessive crossing.

Ex. 24

There are several reasons for this rule. For one thing, it cannot be emphasized too strongly that composition and orchestration are inseparable. That is, the composer must be intimately acquainted with the sounds of each instrument. The learning of counterpoint and harmony is not concerned simply with the manipulation of tones. If we do not write in terms of instrumental or vocal sonorities, our learning will have few practical implications.

Any given vertical interval produces quite a different sound when played by various combinations of instruments, voices, or on the piano. Furthermore, this interval sounds quite different in the various registers or octaves. This may be illustrated by playing the following passage first on the piano and then on various instruments such as two trumpets, two violins, or a flute and a clarinet.

Ex. 25

As can be seen, percussive seconds and other dissonant or consonant intervals change their color when performed on the various instruments. A tenth, for example, which is written for the upper octaves on a piano may be disappointingly thin when performed by two flutes, yet strong again if played by two oboes. Generally speaking, if a thin texture is desired consciously, then wider spacings may be employed, although in the lower registers, wider intervals will tend to be richer and clearer.

Ex. 26

These techniques must be learned through experience, but in the early stages of learning, a maximum of an interval of the tenth is a good rule of the thumb.

The crossing of parts may present similar problems and could well be avoided at this time. If, for example, a viola line crosses below a cello part, we obtain a subtle change in sonority from that produced by the normal disposition of the two instruments. This may be demonstrated in the following example.

Ex. 27

Similar variations of texture may be obtained by other instrumental or vocal interchanges, for example, altos above sopranos or oboes below clarinets, but knowledge of them must be acquired through careful study.

Another reason for avoiding the crossing of parts is that the music's texture may become unintentionally thin at the time of the crossing. If such an effect is desired, then well and good—ignore the rule.

8) Try to avoid simultaneous leaps over the barline.

Ex. 28

Certainly this is no inflexible rule, but we should remember it as it applied to single melody writing. A leap, particularly a large leap, over the barline or from a weak to a strong beat produces a jarring effect which may or may not be intentional. If both voices jump simultaneously to a strong beat, or even to a weak beat, the obvious will result.

It is wise to abide by this rule at first. If one voice leaps from a weak to a strong beat, the other voice should counterbalance this by suspension or by contrary motion by a half or whole step. Of course, if one desires a jagged effect, coupled with the sudden appearance of tension, then simultaneous leaps may be employed, particularly from a consonant to a dissonant interval.

Ex. 29

9) *Exercises may begin and end on any interval.*

There is no necessity, however, for avoiding the more consonant intervals at this time although a dissonance may be effective at the beginning. An examination of the following example illustrates in part the wide choice available.

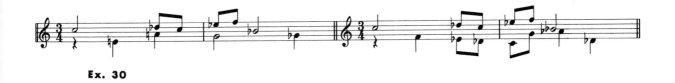

Ex. 30

10) *Try to avoid being a slave of the piano.*

If possible, write the exercises, or at least sections of them, away from the piano, testing them only from time to time. Although it is true that many significant composers use the piano for composing, the inexperienced person may find that too much dependence on the instrument will produce music which is not conceived in terms of orchestral or vocal colors. Furthermore, our ears should have every opportunity to be trained to "hear" melodic lines, intervals and chords on paper, and this is a good time to work on the contemporary phase of this training. Use the piano only when necessary.

RHYTHMIC PROCEDURES In Chapter 1 we discussed the rhythmic problems inherent in melodic writing. When composing for more than one voice, the individual parts must be rhythmically effective, and yet there must be an overall rhythmic pattern produced by the combination of voices.

We mentioned one facet of this when Bach's "cartwheel" technique was discussed (p. 62). The interest inherent in one part should not be obscured by movement in the other. Despite the necessity for creating melodies that possess individual rhythmic interest, there must be a stylistic coordination between the separate lines.

This coordination is not obtained if little rhythmic relationship exists, as in the following example.

Ex. 31

Example 31 would be more effective as follows.

Ex. 32

A simple but effective total pattern is achieved by Walter Piston.

33 Piston *String Quartet No. 4* (p. 14)

Reprinted by permission of Associated Music Publishers, Inc. New York.

A similar pattern is as follows.

34 Hindemith *Mathis der Maler* (p. 34)

It is obvious that polyrhythmic techniques may produce an infinite number of patterns and that these may be achieved through the use of meter changes or dislocated accents. However, at this time it is advisable to use polyrhythms with care, since they can become highly complex—and artificially complex in the hands of an inexperienced composer.

The time-tested pattern of three against two may still be effective.

Ex. 35

Another example of this follows.

Ex. 36

Elliott Carter uses the technique in the following manner.

37 Carter *String Quartet* (1951) (pp. 6–7)
Reprinted by permission of Associated Music Publishers, Inc., New York.

A polyrhythmic passage may lead to a new pattern in which the same rhythm is used in both voices.

Ex. 38

A similar example follows.

Ex. 39

It should be apparent that there is no end to this. Continuous study and writing will enable us to handle more complex patterns with comparative ease. In the beginning, however, relative simplicity may be the better part of wisdom.

HARMONIC RHYTHM The combination of two or more voices must also provide our ears with a sense of harmonic direction through the use of harmonic configurations or patterns that create harmonic rhythm. In traditional music the harmonic rhythm may be static as in the Prelude to Wagner's *Das Rheingold*, in which the waters of the river are symbolized by the continuous use

75

of an E♭ chord. Or the rhythm may be rapid if frequent harmonic changes are employed. In between these two extremes is an infinite number of possible designs, depending upon the mood of the composition.

If, however, we write music that avoids traditional chords, how can we formulate a recognizable harmonic rhythm? When we discuss composition in three or more parts, the procedure will become clearer, but in two-part writing we can still achieve a recognizable harmonic rhythm even if we cannot identify the vertical structures as parts of known triads or higher chords.

For example, in Chapter 1 we spoke of tonal centers within contemporary melodic lines. That is, we said that certain tones may revolve about a note or "key," even though we do not try to identify this "key" as major or minor. If we refer back to Examples 45 and 49 of Chapter 1, we can see that a definable harmonic rhythm may be established within the framework of a single melodic line. It really does not make any difference whether we can determine the exact tonal centers, because such an analysis would be futile in much of our Twentieth-Century music.

Let us now examine another melodic line.

Ex. 40

We have made this intentionally a contrived line in order to clarify this matter. If we perform this melody and do not concern ourselves with the identification of exact tonal centers, we can still hear the harmonic rhythm inherent within the single line. In this rather artificial example note how the rhythm changes with nearly every measure: the first measure consists of "white" notes on the piano which have an obvious relationship with one another, even though any one of these tones might serve as a tonal center; the second measure consists of "black" notes, which introduce a change in the harmonic rhythm; measure three includes both "white" and "black" notes, which are related to two indefinite tonal centers; and the harmonic rhythm changes once more in the final measure.

Now as in traditional composition, harmonic rhythm may become static in contemporary writing or change so rapidly that our ear flounders in a mass of fluctuating sound. When such a rapid harmonic rhythm is used in a single melodic line, "wanderitis" may be the result. If such rhythms are employed in two-part writing, the music may lack a sense of direction. On the other hand, if the harmonic rhythm is too static, the music may simply be dull and lifeless.

Let us return to Example 45 in Chapter 1, using its melody as the basis of a two-part passage. For example, we shall add a bottom voice to this melody.

Andante

Ex. 41

The brackets in Example 41 indicate the various harmonic rhythms: the brackets below the individual lines designate their separate rhythms, and the brackets above indicate the combined rhythm. Note that the harmonic rhythm of the separate lines suggests two individual patterns but that the rhythm of the combined parts assumes a somewhat different shape from that of the individual voices. Thus, if the individual harmonic rhythms are dissimilar, the total pattern will tend to produce a feeling of tension.

Note, for instance, in the following example in which the harmonic rhythm of the lower voice parallels more closely that of the upper part to create a new total pattern which contains less tension.

Ex. 42

The following passage illustrates a kaleidoscopic pattern that is due to excessive chromaticism in the lower voice. The latter wanders haphazardly by half steps and lacks a definable harmonic rhythm, thus diluting the total pattern.

Ex. 43

Paul Hindemith creates a vague harmonic rhythm through a similar use of half steps.

44 Hindemith *First Piano Sonata* (2nd Movement)

Reprinted by permission of B. Schott's Soehne, Mainz, Schott & Co., Ltd., London and Associated Music Publishers, Inc., New York.

But he achieves a clearly perceptible harmonic rhythm in the following excerpt.

45 Hindemith *The Four Temperaments* (p. 19)

Reprinted by permission of B. Schott's Soehne, Mainz, Schott & Co., Ltd., London and Associated Music Publishers, Inc., New York.

Harmonic rhythm, then, remains a vital facet of any compositional style and must be considered carefully if our music is to be effective. Even when we do not work with traditional centers of tonality, we can learn to plot the harmonic rhythm and control it by the force of the individual lines and the careful choice of consonant and dissonant intervals in all of their shadings. Constant practice and listening will increase our understanding.

CONSTRUCTING THE COUNTERPOINT No given cantus firmus will be used, since a centuries-old line would be foreign to our idiom. Furthermore, we should be able to create our own melodic lines now.

However, to help us understand the process of writing in two parts, we will indicate some of the methods that may be used as well as some of the pitfalls that must be avoided. Although most composers may write the two voices at the same time, it may be advisable to compose them successively in the early stages of learning.

Let us assume that we are planning to compose a two-part piece for flute and clarinet and that we have written the following passage for the former instrument.

Ex. 46

This line conforms rather closely to the rules in Chapter 1. There are two leaps in the same direction in measure one, but no traditional chord is outlined, and the melody returns immediately by a half step. There are also skips to the first beats of measures two and three, but the first is a descending skip of the perfect fourth, and as such will not have the force of a leap which ascends. The second skip of a perfect fifth simply emphasizes the high point of the melodic curve. Furthermore, both leaps can be "softened" by the movement of the lower line.

The melodic curve contains interest in that our ears are carried to the high point in the middle and then to a position of rest at the end. The rhythm is simple but effective. In other words, the melody satisfies us, the composer, as being the expression of a certain emotion or feeling, and it is easily playable in the flute's warm lower register.

The lower melodic line for the clarinet must be just as interesting if played alone, and yet when coupled with the flute's part, it must blend stylistically into the whole. Its melodic curve and rhythmic patterns must complement those of the upper voice, and the combined harmonic rhythm of the two parts must be convincing to our ears.

Ex. 47

Following is another example of two-part contrapuntal writing. Check its features against the rules listed in this and the preceding chapter, and if there seem to be discrepancies, try to discover why the rules are broken.

Ex. 48

EXERCISES

1) Go back to the examples of two-part writing included in this chapter and examine them carefully. Perform them in class and listen to the harmonic rhythms and other compositional features. Discuss them in class.

2) Compose short two-part pieces for the following instrumental combinations if they are available in class: two violins, two flutes, two clarinets, two oboes, and two trumpets. Begin with slow tempos and reasonably large note values and write the parts successively. Check each line for its individual effectiveness before it is accepted, since each line must be interesting if played alone.

3) Compose similar pieces for available mixed instrumental combinations such as the following: violin and viola; viola and cello; flute and oboe; oboe and clarinet; flute and clarinet; bassoon and clarinet; bassoon and horn in F.

4) Compose a two-part invention for piano, using Bach's formal schemes without retaining his phrase symmetry. Try to avoid melodic and rhythmic sequences, but be sure that interesting rhythmic patterns exist.

5) Write a two-part composition in small form for two sections of an orchestra or a concert band: violins and violas; violas and cellos; trombones and horns; or mixed combinations as they are available.

6) Select a short poem and write a two-part a cappella work for sopranos and altos or tenors and basses.

7) Compose a similar piece for an a cappella mixed choir with two-part alternating sections.

SCHEDULING SUGGESTIONS

Until two-part writing can be done with comparative ease, it is useless to move on to composition in three or more parts. Certainly no less than one month of intensive study should be spent on this chapter and more could be spent profitably. Student writing should be accompanied by the continuous study of contemporary scores while listening to phonograph recordings.

3 / three-part writing

HARMONIC IMPLICATIONS When a third or a fourth part is added in traditional writing, we are faced with certain problems, but at least we can be guided vertically by our knowledge of tonal harmony. In Twentieth-Century music, however, we are confronted with the added difficulty of handling vertical sounds for which we have no names and with which our ears may not be familiar. To the beginner, this may appear to pose an insuperable problem—but it does not.

Forgetting for the moment the question of rhythm, melodic curves and other compositional matters, let us examine those Twentieth-Century sounds which have little or no relationship to traditional theory and which should not be analyzed in terms of traditional harmony.

In the first place, contemporary chords may be formed by the combination of the three melodic lines and they may become recognizable with use, as were the triads and other traditional chords in past eras. We must remember that the triads, seventh chords, and ninth chords that we label as such in traditional theory were nameless results of counterpoint at one time. Consider, for example, the following three-part writing from the the Thirteenth Century.

1 *Thirteenth-Century Conductus*

In this excerpt we note only two complete triads in the midst of the contrapuntal movement, and these triads are simply the result of the counterpoint. The anonymous composer was unaware of the term "triad." All we can say is that the thirteenth-century composer recognized the fact that an interesting—and by this time a familiar—sound was produced by combining the interval of a perfect fifth with a major and a minor third. As this vertical combination of intervals was used with increasing regularity, it became recognized as an entity within itself.

More than three hundred and fifty years later, the nameless triad had been joined by additional vertical combinations.

2 Gesualdo *Tu m'uccidi, O crudele* (Madrigal)

Here we have a famous example of early Seventeenth Century writing that includes vertical formations later to be accepted as seventh chords, augmented triads, and major and minor triads in their root positions and inversions. Gesualdo explored new sonorities in the same way that many early Twentieth-Century composers coupled contrapuntal lines to produce nameless

87

chords foreign to tonal theory. History has supplied names for Gesualdo's sounds, and perhaps something similar is recurring at this time.

For example, there were no existing harmonic rules to guide Gesualdo in the following sequence of chords.

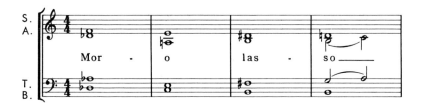

3 Gesualdo *Moro lasso* (Madrigal)

He wrote these chord sequences because he liked their sounds and because they could be achieved through contrapuntal means.

Over the past sixty years, many contemporary composers have explored new sonorities also, and in doing so they have established contrapuntal or harmonic ways of controlling these sounds. In this chapter we are concerned with these contrapuntal methods.

Let us examine a section of three-part writing for viola and piano that is not far removed from traditional writing.

Ex. 4

We see here a passage that avoids traditional chords almost entirely but which must be considered as relatively consonant writing spiced with occasional sharp dissonances. We must resist any tendency to assign traditional tonalities to this music, since, despite the fact that we may hear "incomplete" sevenths, ninths, and other traditional forms, they are the result of the counterpoint and are not intended *per se*.

Now let us examine the following harmonic framework established by the flow of lines.

Ex. 5

Note that the first three-note chord consists of two consonant intervals (perfect fourth and perfect fifth) and one mild dissonance (major second). [Intervals may be calculated without regard to octave extensions.] It is apparent that this chord produces very little tension because the two consonant intervals soften any harshness that results from the mild major second. To Twentieth-Century ears, then, this could be considered a consonant chord which possesses the stability enjoyed by the major or minor triad in the last century.

The following chord is of an almost identical character: two consonant intervals (perfect fourths, which tend to be consonant in dissonant surroundings), which soften the mild dissonance (minor seventh). It should be noted also that these two chords possess two common tones (E♭ and A♭) and that the two moving tones (D♭ and B♭) are closely related. Thus, the movement from one chord to the other will produce little or no harmonic change.

Until we reach the last chord in the first measure, the texture is consonant, owing to the preponderance of consonant intervals. The last chord, however, increases tension, because it contains one sharp dissonance (major seventh), one mild dissonance (major second), and only one consonance (minor third). A chord-by-chord analysis of the entire passage will reveal how the various intervals are combined to produce shadings of tension and relaxation as well as a recognizable harmonic rhythm. It will be noted also that the first two three-note chords analyzed above need no resolution in such a texture, and may, indeed, act in the same capacity as did traditional triads in the last century.

In a consonant passage such as this, we may hear suggested tonal centers, such as A♭ for the first few chords, but none of these chords has a definite tonal name. Such chords may follow each other convincingly and establish various tonal centers only because their intervals are chosen carefully and also because the separate lines are effective. It should be obvious, therefore, that we can obtain a feeling of tension or relaxation by similar techniques as were used by Mozart in a more consonant era.

6 Mozart *Symphony No. 40 in G Minor* (3rd Movement)

Now let us examine a Twentieth-Century example.

7 Hindemith *Ludus Tonalis* *(Arioso)*

Here we see the same mingling of dissonance with consonance in order to create chords which should not be assigned traditional names, even though Hindemith's more conservative style may include occasional traditional triads. The first chord in Example 7 is similar to one we have already discussed: a minor seventh softened by two consonant intervals. Notice, however, how Hindemith introduces tension in the first measure by adding tritones and major seconds (ninths), which overbalance the consonant intervals.

We see, therefore, that the Twentieth-Century composer is very much concerned with harmony, even though he may not think in terms of traditional harmonic forms or sequences. The combination of selected intervals results in consonant and dissonant chords which may become as normal to our ears—and as easy to handle—as the triads and other combinations of preceding centuries. We learn through writing and listening how to couple the various types of intervals to produce these new chords.

For example, if we select middle C as a bottom tone, we may produce series of three-note chords which range from extreme dissonance to relative consonance.

Ex. 8

We have here various combinations of intervals which produce chords—we might just as well say triads—some of which are relatively consonant, some very dissonant, and some lying in between the two extremes. It is obvious, in other words, that such triads formed by two dissonant and one consonant interval will produce more tension than those formed by one dissonant and two consonant intervals. It is obvious, too, that orchestration, dynamics, rhythm, and tempo are contributing factors.

It goes without saying that these forms are not to be memorized, but we will find that constant practice will enable us to employ certain combinations with the knowledge that they will produce desired tensions. We will also learn to "hear" many of these combinations on paper just as we "hear" a traditional triad before it is played.

By choosing our intervals carefully, we can increase or decrease dissonance as in Example 9.

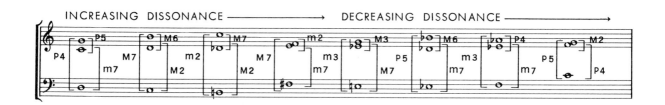

Ex. 9

With meter, rhythm, and dynamic markings, Example 9 might appear as follows.

Andante

Ex. 10

Notice how Paul Hindemith handles increasing and decreasing dissonance in a similar manner.

11 Hindemith *Second Piano Sonata* (p. 18)

Reprinted by permission of B. Schott's Soehne, Mainz, Schott & Co., Ltd., London and Associated Music Publishers, Inc., New York.

We can establish a static harmonic rhythm or one which moves rapidly.

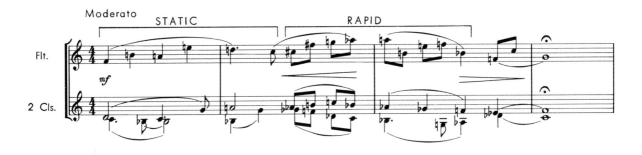

Ex. 12

We may use smaller intervals for their percussive quality and produce a rapid harmonic rhythm.

Ex. 13

Or a fairly static rhythm may be produced with similar spacings.

Ex. 14

OTHER CONSIDERATIONS The rules discussed in Chapters 1 and 2 apply also to three-part writing. For one thing, we must watch our intervals so that fairly uniform distances are preserved, particularly in the middle registers. In general, a good working rule is to keep the inner voice within an octave of the outer voices, although flexibility must be maintained.

Ex. 15

We know, of course, from traditional theory that we must be particularly careful of intervals in the lower registers. If the bottom voice descends below approximately the fourth-line F in the bass clef, it is wise to preserve a distance of at least a perfect fifth between it and the middle line. Otherwise, the musical texture may become cloudy or muddy. The following example avoids this.

Ex. 16

There may be times, however, when closer spacing in the bass register is desired to produce a thicker texture.

Ex. 17

Widely spaced intervals may be employed if the resulting thinness is desired.

Ex. 18

Remember that the individual movement of each line should not be obscured by continuous movement in the other voices. Keep Bach's "cartwheel" principle firmly in mind.

Ex. 19

Continue to strive for contrary motion, particularly between the outer voices, although this should be relieved by some parallel and similar motion.

Ex. 20

We now have three melodic curves to watch, although the one in the highest voice remains the most important, owing to its exposed position. However, try to establish three dissimilar curves so that the individual high points do not coincide. Such dissimilarity tends to make the music more exciting through the appearances of the individual high points. In a quiet passage, however, successive climaxes might disturb the overall mood.

Keep the rhythmic patterns interesting, but avoid complexities in the first exercises. If contrasting meters are desired, be sure that the same effect cannot be obtained more logically by employing dislocated accents.

Ex. 21

COMPOSITIONAL PROCEDURES In order to illustrate the various points explained above, let us construct a short section of three-part counterpoint for violin, viola, and cello. First, we shall compose the bass line according to the rules in Chapter 1.

Ex. 22

Now let us add the middle voice, which should be in accord with both the rules in Chapter 1 and the rules for two-part writing discussed in Chapter 2.

Ex. 23

Finally we can add the top line.

Ex. 24

First, let us examine the harmonic rhythm. We should notice that it changes in a clearly perceptible pattern throughout the entire passage. The first two measures are fairly static but slight harmonic fluctuations create interest. From the third measure through the end, however, the harmonic rhythm moves effectively. Only in measure five do sharp dissonances cloud the pattern momentarily.

In general, the passage is consonant. A♭ and D♭ tonal centers are suggested in the first two measures, and other tonal centers are heard clearly in the passage, although only two traditional triads actually appear: an E♭ minor triad in measure three and a G♭ minor triad in measure five. All chords, including the two traditional triads, result from the movement of the separate lines and the careful selection of intervals. Each line could stand alone.

The total rhythmic pattern is simple, yet interesting, and the movement of the individual lines is never obscured by that of the other parts. Duple meter is introduced in the lowest line without resorting to meter changes.

The melodic curves are rather similar, but the three individual high points are heard in succession so as to create a series of climaxes. Although there is a tendency toward parallel movement between the outer lines, there is enough contrary motion, perhaps, to introduce linear individuality.

The spacing of the lines is good and the eight measures will "sound" on the instruments for which they were written. The total effect is clear and smooth.

Let us now examine another example, written by the same procedures as Example 24.

Ex. 25

Play this example in class on the designated instruments (bass clarinet may be substituted for bassoon) and check to see whether it is in accord with the following rules:

1) each voice should be an independent melody which outlines no traditional chords directly, and yet does not include arbitrary accidentals and leaps.

2) each voice should contain an interesting melodic curve which avoids equal high and low points.

3) the three lines should be similar in style, but the individual curves should be dissimilar.

4) each voice should lie well for its designated instrument.

5) the distance between the voices should produce a clear sonority.

6) the movement of no voice should be obscured by that of the others.

7) the rhythm of each part should be interesting, and the three lines should combine to produce an effective total pattern.

8) leaps in each voice should be balanced by movement in the other parts, particularly if the leaps are from weak to strong beats.

9) there should be an effective mixture of tension and relaxation produced by chords which vary from consonance to extreme dissonance.

10) the harmonic rhythm should change in a discernible pattern.

It should be apparent that slavish attention to each of the points listed above is not likely to produce a world-shaking musical masterpiece, but the points are still valid. Great creative minds may stretch these rules or ignore a few of them, but our knowledge of them is essential if we are to have a profound understanding of almost any musical age.

At this time, it is advisable to continue composing each voice separately in order to avoid stereotyped melodic lines. Compose either the bottom or the top voice first and then add the middle and the remaining outer part. When adding the third voice, it may be necessary to alter certain tones in the two other parts, but remember that each line should be an effective melodic line that can stand alone. If there is a choice between the horizontal and vertical lines, the former should be considered more important.

EXERCISES

1) Compose short three-part pieces for the following instruments as they are available in class: two violins and a viola; violin, viola, and cello; flute, oboe, and clarinet (substitute a clarinet or flute for the oboe if necessary); oboe (clarinet), clarinet, and bassoon (or bass clarinet); clarinet, horn in F, and bassoon; two trumpets and a trombone; trumpet, horn, and trombone. Compose the lowest line first, following it with the middle voice.

2) Compose other short pieces for the instrumental combinations listed in Exercise 1, but write the highest voice first, following it with either one of the remaining parts.

3) Compose a three-part invention for piano following Bach's general form but

avoiding his melodic and rhythmic sequences.

4) Choose a poetic text and write a three-part choral work for unaccompanied women's voices. Utilize a contrapuntal texture.

5) Select a religious text and compose a short hymn in syllabic style, beginning and ending on chords composed of two consonant and one mild dissonant interval. Passing tones may be employed, but keep the rhythm and texture simple.

6) Compose a longer work for three available instruments. Thin the texture at times to two voices.

7) Follow the procedure suggested in Exercise 6 and write a short piece for chamber orchestra or small concert band.

SCHEDULING SUGGESTIONS

Continue to study scores and use them while listening to phonograph recordings. Discuss all examples listed in this chapter in class. Perform all student exercises in class and discuss them, also.

One to two months of intensive three-part writing should allow the student to progress to the next chapter. Under normal circumstances, the first three chapters may be completed during the first half of a school year if there are no less than three meetings each week.

4 / *composition in four or more parts*

TEXTURE The rules and procedures discussed in the first three chapters apply also to composition involving four or more voices. The major problem is again harmonic, since there are added intervals to watch.

As in traditional writing, our vertical combinations may contain four or more different tones or doublings which produce chords with two or more notes. Our choice is limited merely by the texture desired and by the direction of the individual lines.

If, for example, we wish to emphasize a dissonant tone, we may double it as follows.

Ex. 1

Or if we wish to enrich the texture, we may double one or more tones at the octave.

Ex. 2

As in three-part writing, we should maintain a fairly even distance between the separate lines if we wish to achieve clarity.

Ex. 3

Igor Stravinsky accomplishes this in choral writing as follows.

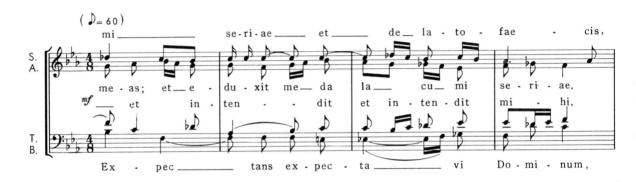

4 **Stravinsky** *Symphony of Psalms* **(2nd Movement)**
Copyright 1931 by Russischer Musikverlag; renewed 1958. Copyright and renewal assigned to Boosey & Hawkes Inc. Revised Edition Copyright 1948 by Boosey and Hawkes Inc. Reprinted by permission.

And Paul Hindemith achieves this clarity in piano writing.

5 Hindemith *First Piano Sonata* (4th Movement)

Reprinted by permission of B. Schott's Soehne, Mainz, Schott and Co., Ltd., London and Associated Publishers, Inc., New York.

There may be times, however, when a thicker texture is desired.

Ex. 6

A similar texture is achieved by Arnold Schoenberg in the following example.

7 Schoenberg *Pierrot Lunaire (Gebet an Pierrot)*
Reprinted by permission of Universal Edition A. G., Vienna and Associated Music Publishers Inc., New York.

We may thin out the texture by the temporary elimination of voices and through the use of more widely spaced intervals.

116

Ex. 8

Hindemith produces a similar texture in the following manner.

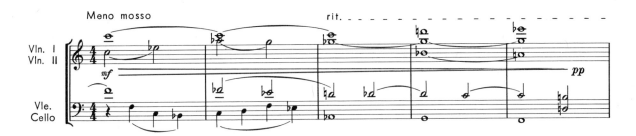

9 Hindemith *Sixth String Quartet* (p. 8)
Reprinted by permission of B. Schott's Soehne, Mainz, Schott & Co., Ltd., London and Associated Music Publishers, Inc., New York.

HARMONIC IMPLICATIONS Twentieth-Century chords consisting of four or more different tones are formed exactly as were the three-note forms discussed in Chapter 3: Tension is in proportion to the number and kind of dissonant and consonant intervals employed. As we noted in the last chapter, two consonant intervals tend to soften a mild dissonance (major second or minor seventh) and produce a chord that is stable and in no need of resolution.

It is obvious that this principle is continued and extended when we deal with additional voices. Examine, for instance, the following chords, which may be considered consonant by Twentieth-Century standards. Note also that this sequence of chords could be utilized as the framework for a short piece.

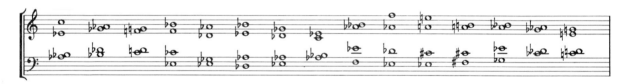

Ex. 10

If, however, we wish to add more tension to our music, we might mix consonant chords with those in which sharp and mild dissonances tend to overbalance the more consonant intervals. In this light, analyze the following four-note combinations.

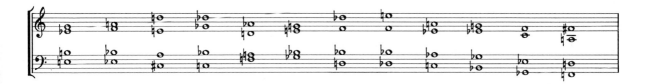

Ex. 11

Extremely dissonant chords may be constructed as follows.

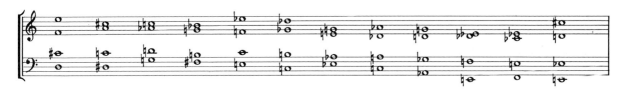

Ex. 12

The chords illustrated in Examples 10, 11, and 12 are only a few of those available to us and depend solely upon the tension or lack of tension we desire. They may be created by the movement of our individual lines or without reference to horizontal movement. At this

119

time, however, we are concerned primarily with contrapuntal considerations which enable us to handle consonant and dissonant shadings with comparative ease.

As an extension of this, chords containing more than four different tones may be constructed in the same manner in order to produce the desired degrees of tension.

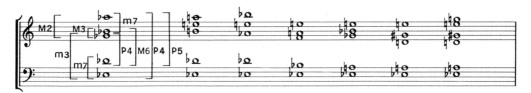

Ex. 13

It follows, therefore, that if the separate lines of the music are convincing and if the spacing of intervals is handled effectively, we may achieve a harmonic pattern capable of producing any kind of mood. In the following example, the over-all pattern is relatively consonant, and the harmonic rhythm is clearly discernible.

120

String
Quartet

Ex. 14

Sharp dissonance may be mixed with consonance.

4 Horns

Ex. 15

Note, for example, how Paul Hindemith writes a passage in which the consonance of one measure flows into a more dissonant section and then back into relative consonance.

16 Hindemith *Mathis der Maler* (p. 17)

Reprinted by permission of B. Schott's Soehne, Mainz, Schott & Co., Ltd., London and Associated Music Publishers, Inc., New York.

We see that the mild tension employed by Hindemith results from the use of soft dissonances tempered by consonant intervals.

With Schoenberg, however, we encounter added tension from the increased use of sharp dissonances, although they, too, are tempered by mild dissonances and consonances.

17 Schoenberg *Fourth String Quartet* (p. 18)

Copyright, 1939, by G. Schirmer, Inc. Reprinted by permission.

Notice in the following harmonic framework of Example 17 how Schoenberg begins with a perfect fifth and carefully adds tension by using mild dissonances, followed in turn by sharply dissonant intervals, after which there is a release from tension.

18 Schoenberg *Fourth String Quartet* (Harmonic Framework)

Copyright, 1939, by G. Schirmer, Inc. Reprinted by permission.

As we know, however, from previous discussion, our choice of harmonic rhythms is of the utmost importance. Thus, we are concerned not only with the texture of the music and the tension desired, but also with the pace of our harmony. This pace or rhythm may be rapid, static, or somewhere in between.

For example, Walter Piston chooses a rather static harmonic rhythm for the following example.

19 Piston *String Quartet No. 4* (p. 10)
Reprinted by permission of Associated Music Publishers, Inc., New York.

The harmonic rhythm is rapid in the next passage, however, owing to the many half steps used in the four lines.

20 Piston *String Quartet No. 4* (p. 15)
Reprinted by permission of Associated Music Publishers Inc., New York.

The chromatic bass in the following excerpt produces rapid harmonic changes.

21 Hindemith *Sixth String Quartet* (p. 6)
Reprinted by permission of B. Schott's Soehne, Mainz, Schott & Co., Ltd., London and Associated Music Publishers, Inc., New York.

Hindemith, in the next example, produces a slower harmonic rhythm through the use of diatonic lines.

126

22 Hindemith *The Four Temperaments* (p. 1)

Reprinted by permission of B. Schott's Soehne, Mainz, Schott & Co., Ltd., London and Associated Music Publishers, Inc., New York.

RHYTHMIC PROBLEMS In multi-voiced composition, the problems of rhythm can be considerable. The natural tendency for many beginning composers is to construct intricate rhythmic patterns, which not only hide the movement of the individual lines but which also impede the progress of the total rhythmic flow. In the beginning stages of study it would be well to retain some simplicity without forsaking rhythmic interest.

Note, for example, how Hindemith produces an interesting effect by shifting the rhythmic pattern in a simple passage that might have become tediously repetitious.

23 Hindemith *Symphony in E♭* (p. 1)
Reprinted by permission of B. Schott's Soehne, Mainz, Schott & Co., Ltd., London and Associated Music Publishers, Inc., New York.

In the following example, he employs a meter change, adding interest to a basically simple pattern.

24 Hindemith *Symphony in E♭* (p. 6)

Reprinted by permission of B. Schott's Soehne, Mainz, Schott & Co., Ltd., London and Associated Music Publishers, Inc., New York.

Meter changes make the following passage effective.

25 Stravinsky *Three Pieces for String Quartet* (p. 1)

Copyright 1922 by Edition Russe de Musique. All rights assigned to Boosey and Hawkes Inc. Reprinted by permission.

But we must remember that meter changes are not always necessary or as effective as displacing the beat by ties over the barlines. Notice how Bartók produces interest by shifting the accents in the various lines.

26 Bartók *Fifth String Quartet* (p. 71)

In the following passage Bartók introduces duple meter in one measure to break the regular six-eight meter flow.

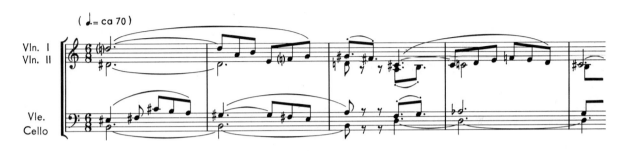

27 Bartók *Sixth String Quartet* (p. 3)
Copyright 1941 by Hawkes and Son (London) Ltd. Reprinted by permission of Boosey and Hawkes Inc.

COMPOSITIONAL PROCEDURES The problems of rhythm, melodic curves, and effective melodic lines in four- or more-part writing are identical with those of music with fewer voices. Care must be taken to retain the individuality of each line, but all parts must be written in a similar style. The rhythmic flow must not be haphazard; a general pattern should be discernible.

Let us outline the steps that might be followed at this time in writing for four voices.

First, we may compose an effective melody for the top voice.

Ex. 28

Next we may write the second line from the top.

Ex. 29

Now we may add a third voice.

Ex. 30

And last we may compose the lowest part.

Ex. 31

134

Here, then, is an uncomplicated passage which illustrates the comparatively consonant style we are using at this time. Rhythmically it is simple but flowing, and the individual movement of each voice is heard clearly, except, perhaps, in the third measure. Each line has its own melodic curve, although all high points tend to merge in measures three and four, a characteristic that may weaken the passage somewhat. Skips over the barlines are balanced by the movement of other voices to eliminate unintentional roughness. All intervals are spaced for clarity.

Harmonically, the passage is conservative without employing traditional forms except for a momentary D-minor triad in the fourth measure. Incomplete ninth chords and a triad with added sixth also occur, but all vertical forms—combinations of consonant and dissonant intervals—are generated by the movement of the four voices. Sharp dissonances appear occasionally to create tension. The harmonic rhythm is rapid with changes on nearly every beat, except in the next to the last measure. However, many of the changes are slight, so that the total harmonic picture is not kaleidoscopic.

As we have said, this method of successive counterpoint is not always the procedure followed, but if the beginning student works with all four voices at the same time, the individual lines may suffer in the attempt to find effective vertical sonorities. After some time we should attempt a combination of successive and simultaneous counterpoint.

EXERCISES

1) Compose a short piece for string quartet, varying the four-part writing with sections in two and three-part counterpoint. Keep the individual lines interesting and maintain a fairly consonant texture, using accented and unaccented sharp dissonances to increase the tension at certain points. Watch the spacing of the intervals and be careful not to allow the two lower voices to crowd together in the low register of the viola.

2) Compose a short composition for available woodwinds, preferably flute, oboe, clarinet, and bassoon.

3) Compose a short work for string orchestra and include two-, three-, and four-part sections. Double the cello with string basses at the lower octave or in unison, except in passages where a thinner texture is desired.

4) Choose a short contemporary poem and compose a four-part madrigal for mixed voices. Thin the texture at times by omitting one or more voices.

5) Select another short poem and write a song for soprano or baritone with an accompaniment of violin, viola, and cello; if these instruments are not available, write the accompaniment for three woodwinds.

SCHEDULING SUGGESTIONS

Scores and phonograph recordings should be assigned for individual study purposes and some representative works may be heard and discussed in class.

Three to five weeks of serious study should be spent on this chapter.

5 / contrapuntal devices

A study of contemporary compositions written in any style will illustrate the fact that the Twentieth-Century composer may utilize any contrapuntal technique or form that will enable him to present his ideas. In other words, all of the practices of pre-Twentieth-Century contrapuntal writing may be employed: imitation, augmentation, diminution, pedal points, ostinato figures, canons, fugues, and others.

For example, Arnold Schoenberg uses imitation as follows.

1 Schoenberg *Three Piano Pieces,* Op. 11, No. 1
Reprinted by permission of Universal Edition A. G. Vienna and Associated Music Publishers, Inc., New York.

Hindemith also employs imitation.

2 Hindemith *Mathis der Maler* (p. 19)
Reprinted by permission of B. Schott's Soehne, Mainz, Schott & Co., Ltd., London and Associated Music Publishers, Inc., New York.

In general, however, one might say that most contemporary composers are careful not to overuse imitation, or, like Schoenberg in Example 1, they tend to veil it by rhythmic shifts. An excessive use of melodic or rhythmic imitation may make the music tedious.

Canonic writing is also used a great deal by contemporary composers. An example of an extremely simple style is as follows:

Moderato

Ex. 3

A more complex canonic section is seen in the following example.

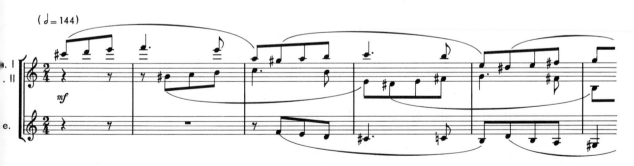

4 Bartók *Fifth String Quartet* (p. 72)

The ostinato-type bass is also used frequently, but it may be more effective if there are written or implied meter changes.

Ex. 5

Hindemith employs a similar ostinato technique without employing meter changes.

6 Hindemith *Second Piano Sonata* (1st Movement)

Reprinted by permission of B. Schott's Soehne, Mainz, Schott & Co., Ltd. London and Associated Music Publishers, Inc., New York.

Another time-tested device that may be used is called "melodic doubling." This is, of course, a technique as old as Western polyphonic music. Although the device is not contrapuntal in itself, it may still be employed in contrapuntal—or harmonic—music to produce interesting sonorities. Any melodic line may be doubled at any interval. Thus, thirds and sixths may be used as follows:

Ex. 7

And again, as follows:

Ex. 8

Anton Webern uses thirds and sixths, also.

9 Webern *Five Pieces for String Quartet* (pp. 1–2)

Reprinted by permission of Universal Edition A. G., Vienna and Associated Music Publishers, Inc., New York.

142

Two lines of doubled thirds may be employed in contrary motion.

Ex. 10

One line of doubled thirds may be used against another line of mixed intervals.

11 **Hindemith** *First Piano Sonata* **(4th Movement)**

Reprinted by permission of B. Schott's Soehne, Mainz, Schott & Co., Ltd., London and Associated Music Publishers, Inc., New York.

A melodic line may be doubled at the ninth and second.

Ex. 12

Or two lines of mixed intervals may be used in contrary motion.

13 Hindemith *First Piano Sonata* (2nd Movement)

These are, of course, mere extensions of traditional practice, and the variations are infinite. We must be aware of the fact, however, that melodic doubling may lead to musical clichés which negate the principle of melodic invention. For the most part, melodic doubling is useful as a color agent and should be used sparingly.

THE FUGUE The Twentieth-Century fugue follows approximately the same pattern as that used in preceding centuries. It is obvious that the words "tonal" and "real" may have no significance in non-tonal music. While modern composers write answers at any interval, we may be wise to compose our answers a fifth above or a fourth below and delay subtleties for some time.

As in traditional writing, the fugue subject must contain some rhythmic or melodic element that will be effective as a recognizable developmental feature. The subject, of course, may be of any length, although a short subject will be more manageable in the early stages of learning.

Since the fugue is a style and not a form, its composition must be left to the discretion of the composer. There is no reason, however, why the contemporary fugue can not have the usual episodes, stretto, and other features inherent within this style. From the standpoint of study, the student is advised to examine Hindemith's *Ludus Tonalis* with its twelve fugues and interludes for piano.

The beginning of Hindemith's *Fuga quarta in A* is as follows.

With energy (♩=108)

14 Hindemith *Ludus Tonalis (Fuga quarta in A)*

Reprinted by permission of B. Schott's Soehne, Mainz, Schott & Co., Ltd., London and Associated Music Publishers, Inc., New York.

Hindemith employs inversion as follows.

(♩=108)

15 Hindemith *Ludus Tonalis (Fuga quarta in A)*

Reprinted by permission of B. Schott's Soehne, Mainz, Schott & Co., Ltd., London and Associated Music Publishers, Inc., New York.

A stretto is used in the following manner.

16 Hindemith *Ludus Tonalis (Fuga quarta in A)*
Reprinted by permission of B. Schott's Soehne, Mainz, Schott & Co., Ltd., London and Associated Music Publishers, Inc., New York.

The next example illustrates a stretto containing retrograde and retrograde inversion.

147

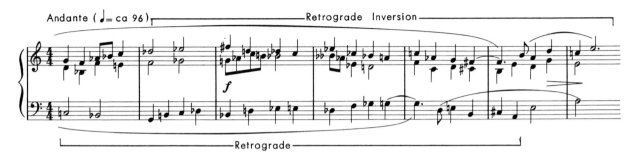

17 Hindemith *Ludus Tonalis (Fuga tertia in F)*

As we can see, the main difference between a Twentieth-Century fugue and one by J. S. Bach may be the choice of intervals. The style may be dissonant or consonant. The basic need is for a subject that has rhythmic and melodic individuality.

Ex. 18

Notice that this subject contains several melodic-rhythmic patterns that may be used developmentally in various ways.

Ex. 19

The answer in the second voice may be as follows.

149

Ex. 20

      Notice above that the "cartwheel" principle is employed enabling us to hear the individual rhythms of each voice. Furthermore, each melodic curve is dissimilar and the high points do not coincide. The intervals shade from consonance to extreme dissonance. Note also how the original three-measure phrase is extended in order to avoid symmetry and how rhythmic figurations in the subject have been used in the upper voice.

      The third voice appears as follows (with a two-measure extension).

Ex. 21

The fourth line is added as follows.

Ex. 22

A four-measure episode based on two of the subject's motives is written.

Ex. 23

The first two measures of the subject are inverted a perfect fourth higher.

Ex. 24

A stretto is used in which the subject is seen in its original form in the bass, in augmentation in the top voice, and inverted in the middle part.

Ex. 25

153

These fugal procedures are in general accord with those employed by composers during the last two centuries. The Twentieth-Century composer may follow them freely and choose a consonant or dissonant idiom. The choice is his.

EXERCISES

1) Compose a short fugue for flute, clarinet, and bassoon (or bass clarinet) with episodes and simple stretto. Introduce the subject in the lowest part and answer it a perfect fifth higher in the clarinet line, extending the answer one or two measures before the entrance of the flute. Remember that each line must be interesting in itself.

2) Compose a short three-voice fugue for piano using procedures similar to those employed in Exercise 1.

3) Compose a fugue of any length for string quartet or woodwind ensemble consisting of instruments available in class. Introduce the subject in the top voice and utilize melodic and rhythmic motives within the subject for developmental purposes in augmentation, diminution, inversion, and retrograde.

4) Write a short four-voice piece for two flutes, two oboes (or clarinets), two clarinets, and two bassoons (or bass clarinets) in which various types of melodic doubling are used. The different pairs may be used to double each of the four parts at an interval, or two lines may be doubled with four-note chords. If three lines are to be doubled, use two bassoons (or bass clarinets) for the lowest line, two clarinets and one oboe (or

third clarinet) for the middle voice, and one oboe (or a fourth clarinet) and two flutes for the upper line.

Four lines may be doubled as follows.

Ex. 26

Melodic doubling of three lines may be as follows.

Ex. 27

And two lines may be doubled in the following manner.

Ex. 28

SCHEDULING SUGGESTIONS

One month or less should provide sufficient time for study of this chapter. Since fugue writing is a very specialized art in itself, it is doubtful whether the average student preparing himself as a performer, teacher, listener, or conductor should spend as much time on this subject as on the other aspects of composition discussed in this book. Certainly all musicians should understand these contrapuntal techniques, and the composer, in particular, should know them well, but there are, perhaps, more important facets of contemporary composition which should be understood by all.

6 / *increasing dissonance*

The first five chapters of this book have urged care in the use of dissonance and in the composition of melodic lines. If we were to end our studies here, however, we would remain ignorant of a great body of Twentieth-Century music which follows a more dissonant path.

History has already italicized its quota of this music, and those compositions which are being written now will have their own assessment at a later date. We should understand this body of music—significant and insignificant—and furthermore, this understanding would allow us to comprehend the reason for newer developments such as *musique concrète*, electronic music, and composition utilizing microtones, even though these developments do not come within the scope of this book.

There are innumerable composers who prefer to use a more dissonant style which seems to reflect the present spirit of the times.

The great majority of these men and women are sincere composers who realize that their course leads to comparative loneliness; "radicals" are shunned by most publishers and nearly all conductors, performers, and audiences. This, however, is the history of music being enacted on a larger scale in the Twentieth Century.

Whereas many of these composers prefer to use serial techniques in some form or another, others object to the "confinement" inherent (to them) in such a style. Nevertheless both groups may achieve much the same end in terms of sound. The choice, as always, remains a personal matter. As musicians or intelligent listeners, we should become thoroughly acquainted with all of these practices. Ears soon become accustomed to new sounds, and hands become practiced at putting them down on paper. Creative inspiration is another matter.

NON-SERIAL COMPOSITION This chapter is concerned with composition in which a predominantly dissonant style is achieved without using any form or variation of the twelve-tone technique. We shall see that such a style (or styles) is merely an extension of the more conservative idioms discussed in the previous chapters in that a composer may choose to employ more sharply dissonant melodic and harmonic intervals. The main difference between this more dissonant idiom and the one we have studied may be the concept—or absence—of the melodic line, as we shall see.

MELODIC TYPES Some of the rules listed in Chapter 1 remain valid; some must be altered or extended; others have no validity. The melodic line in highly dissonant music may flow smoothly or it may be fragmented in various ways. For example, a composer may choose to employ a succession of half steps.

Ex. 1

Such a melodic line tends to be used to produce particular sonorities, because it revolves about clusters of small melodic intervals which may result in a static harmonic rhythm. The line in Example 1 revolves around the following clusters.

Ex. 2

The melodic line in a more dissonant idiom may, however, consist of a variety of melodic intervals.

Ex. 3

A melody like this one possesses more directional force through the combination of small and large intervals.

If we wish to make our line even more forceful, we may include larger leaps.

4. Webern *Five Pieces for String Quartet* (pp. 1–2)
Reprinted by permission of Universal Edition A. G., Vienna and Associated Music Publishers, Inc., New York.

Webern's lines in Example 5 make considerable demands upon a singer and instrumentalists.

161

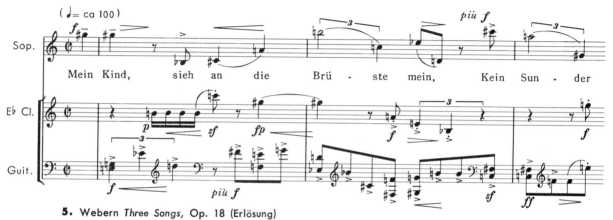

5. Webern *Three Songs,* Op. 18 (Erlösung)

Reprinted by permission of Universal Edition A. G., Vienna and Associated Music Publishers, Inc., New York.

Example 5 illustrates the displacement of the octave within a melodic line. The following is another example of this linear style.

6. Carter *String Quartet* (1951) (pp. 4–5)

Reprinted by permission of Associated Music Publishers, Inc., New York.

There are, perhaps, two main reasons for such a melodic style. In the first place, if we refer back to Example 2 in Chapter 1, which illustrates the subject of Beethoven's *Great Fugue*, we see that other composers have wished to impart a nervous quality to their music through the use of disjointed melodic lines. There may also be the desire to explore the various colors inherent in an instrument's or voice's entire range. The sonorities obtained in this manner have attracted many composers.

However, one must not think that the composer first writes the melody within the confines of one octave and then displaces it. If, for example, we transpose Elliott Carter's line of Example 6 to a common octave, it would appear as follows.

7. Carter *String Quartet* (1951) (pp. 4–5)
Reprinted by permission of Associated Music Publishers, Inc., New York.

In this form, the line is singularly unexciting. But Carter's sensitive ear was able to hear the more effective line as he distributed the notes among the various strings and registers of the cello.

We may note, however, that the melodic intervals in Example 6 are quite consonant and that there is a tendency for the line to return after one or two leaps in the same direction. Furthermore, a distinct melodic curve is present, reaching its single high point in the first measure.

An examination of these distinctive lines employed in highly dissonant compositions reveals the fact that some of the rules in Chapter 1 are still valid. It is obvious, for example, that traditional chords are foreign to this idiom and are seldom employed except as passing chords on weak beats or they may be obscured by other harmonic or contrapuntal features of the music.

Furthermore, if a smoothly dissonant style is desired, leaps from weak to strong beats, unless used with care, may still disturb the flow of the music. If we prefer to employ octave displacements, then the rule has no validity.

We should continue to avoid repeating a note on strong beats of nearby measures or using the same tone too frequently in a short melody. These tend to introduce monotony in any style. For similar reasons, we should still avoid equal high and low points, whether our idiom is smooth or jagged.

We must continue to handle rhythmic patterns with care and to avoid using the same pattern in consecutive or adjacent measures. Furthermore, symmetry is normally avoided and four- and eight-measure phrases may be less effective than those with an uneven number of measures. Phrase extensions and rhythmic displacements are effective also, but we must continue to be careful to avoid artificialities in our music.

TWO-PART WRITING To utilize such varied melodic lines as a basis for two-part composition adds no insuperable problems. We must still consider carefully the sonorities created by the distance between the two lines and the shades of consonance and dissonance used. The two parts may be coupled contrapuntally or in other ways. We shall examine the various techniques.

CONTRAPUNTAL PROCEDURES If our music is to preserve a smooth but dissonant texture, we will naturally avoid octave displacements and use smaller melodic intervals interspersed with occasional skips for added interest and direction. If we are striving more for color than for melodic force, we may use a majority of small melodic intervals in one or both of the parts.

Ex. 8

Color may also be produced by employing two lines of melodic doubling.

165

Ex. 9

If, however, we wish to maintain more of a balance between color and melodic interest in a flowing texture, we may prefer to use some larger melodic intervals, including leaps. It might also be noted that a constant diet of minor seconds, major sevenths, and tritones can provide monotonous fare. We should not lose sight of the fact that major seconds, minor sevenths, and consonant intervals have not been outlawed—just outnumbered. Note the following interchange of consonant and dissonant intervals.

Ex. 10

166

11 Alban Berg *Lyric Suite* (p. 11)

Reprinted by permission of Associated Music Publishers, Inc., New York.

Even if we employ octave displacements, we may still wish to retain a contrapuntal style with both lines displaying individual melodic characteristics yet complementing each other.

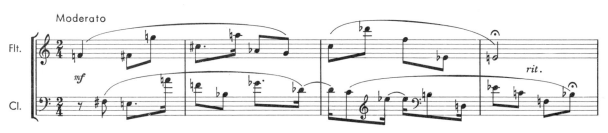

Ex. 12

Melodic doubling of any kind may be employed in this more jagged idiom.

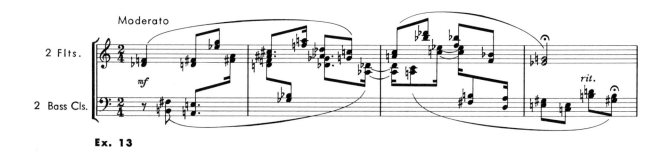

Ex. 13

COMPOSITION FOR THREE OR MORE VOICES When composers of highly dissonant music use more than two lines, their technique is simply an extension of that used in two-part writing. The composer is still extremely conscious of the combination of vertical intervals in order to provide controlled shadings of dissonance and relative consonance. Such music may be written in any style: chromatically flowing or jagged, employing octave displacements and other techniques. Contrapuntal practices may be followed, or the composer may seek desired sonorities which result from a more vertical style of writing.

A four-part dissonant composition may be developed by contrapuntal methods with each line retaining its own individuality while blending into the whole.

Ex. 14

Roger Sessions writes as follows in this style.

15 Sessions *Quintet* (1958) (pp. 3–4)

Reprinted by permission of Edward B. Marks Music Corporation, New York.

In the next example, however, there is an increased emphasis on sonority produced by the preponderance of half steps in the various lines.

Ex. 16

A contrapuntally dissonant style may be used for choral writing, but unless we have access to a select choir consisting of members with perfect pitch, the temptation to employ octave displacements might well be resisted. However, if the separate lines move mainly in a scalewise manner with occasional skips, such music may be sung by any competent group.

Ex. 17

Alban Berg demands the following in a vocalization for male chorus.

18 Berg Wozzeck (Act II. Scene Four)

Reprinted by permission of Universal Edition A.G., Vienna and Associated Music Publishers, Inc., New York.

If a more jagged effect is desired in instrumental writing, wider skips and octave displacements may be used. The vertical intervals, however, should be calculated carefully.

19 Webern *Five Pieces for String Quartet,* Op. 5 (p. 4)

Reprinted by permission of Universal Edition A. G., Vienna and Associated Music Publishers, Inc., New York.

In piano writing, this style may be as follows.

20 Schoenberg *Three Piano Pieces,* Op. 11, No. 1

Reprinted by permission of Universal Edition A. G., Vienna and Associated Music Publishers, Inc., New York.

Elliott Carter uses a combination of flowing and jagged lines in the following passage.

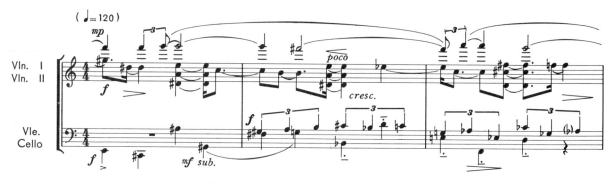

21 Carter *String Quartet* (1951) (p. 5)
Reprinted by permission of Associated Music Publishers, Inc., New York.

A melodic line may be accompanied by dissonant chords.

22 Schoenberg *Three Piano Pieces*, Op. 11, No. 1

Reprinted by permission of Universal Edition A. G., Vienna and Associated Music Publishers, Inc., New York.

Or a melodic line may be harmonized as follows in block harmonies constructed of dissonant and consonant intervals.

23 Schoenberg *Three Piano Pieces*, Op. 11, No. 2

Reprinted by permission of Universal Edition A. G., Vienna and Associated Music Publishers, Inc., New York.

Ostinato accompaniments may be employed.

Ex. 24

POINTILLISM Many contemporary composers, whether they employ serial techniques or not, fragment their melodic lines by dividing them between two or more voices. Such an offshoot or extension of octave displacement may be illustrated as follows.

Ex. 25

As developed mainly by Anton Webern, such a style is reminiscent rhythmically of the medieval *hoquetus* or hocket technique, seen in the two upper voices of the next example.

(Amen)

26 Machaut Mass *(Gloria)*

In the Twentieth Century, this technique allows a composer to explore an even wider range of sonorities and rhythmic complexities. It depends largely on the esthetic force of measured silences, highly contrasting dynamics, and extremely wide intervallic distances. A clear example of this fragmented style is seen in the following excerpt.

177

27 Webern *Variations for Orchestra*, Op. 30 (p. 1)

Reprinted by permission of Universal Edition A. G., Vienna and Associated Music Publishers, Inc., New York.

Example 27 reveals concisely the contemporary interest in sonorities: the momentary shafts of contrasting color produced by the alternation of string bass, oboe, and viola in combination, followed by melodic bits for trombone, violins, and cellos. If such a musical concept seems farfetched, we should go back once again in history for examples.

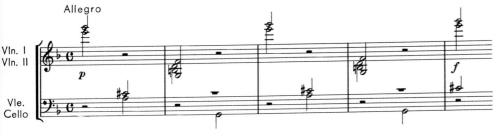

Ex. 28 Beethoven *String Quartet in F*, Op. 59, No. 1

It does not take a great deal of imagination to see that Beethoven was exploring the same realm of sound.

The following example of Twentieth-Century pointillism illustrates a more sustained style.

29 Webern *String Quartet,* Op. 28 (p. 7)

Reprinted by permission of Universal Edition, A. G., Vienna and Associated Music Publishers, Inc., New York.

We should note in Examples 27 and 29 that consonant intervals have not been eliminated from this idiom. Webern uses them to balance the more dissonant intervals. Note, too, the careful use of dynamic markings and accent marks which add to the total effect. It must be remembered that such music is not conceived in a common octave and then transposed. The composer must "hear" these fragmented sounds before putting them down on paper.

Finally, let us examine the more complex style employed by Karlheinz Stockhausen.

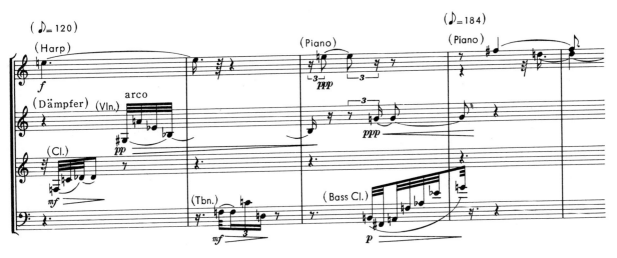

31 Stockhausen *Nr. 1 "Kontra-Punkte"* (p. 33)
Reprinted by permission of Universal Edition (London) Ltd. and Associated Music Publishers, Inc., New York.

It should be obvious that such a technique in the hands of inexperienced composers may produce artificial results. But this is true of any technique, whether it is concerned with simple traditional harmony or with pointillism. To condemn melodic fragmentation or any other contemporary idioms *per se* is to be unaware of history. Such an idiom—whether one likes or dislikes it—has firm roots in the past. Its complex rhythms spring from Beethoven, Berlioz, and their significant contemporaries; its philosophy of sonority has its roots in the Nineteenth Century; its jagged lines and exploration of extended registers stem from the ages; and its dissonance lies rooted firmly in all centuries.

Such fragmentation, however, has tended to lead to the production of sounds by new means: electronic music and *musique concrète*, in which intricate rhythms and complex textures can be prepared on magnetic tape. In this way, the problems inherent in human performance are avoided: the high cost of long rehearsals, the relative scarcity of virtuoso instrumentalists and singers, the frailty of the human ear, and other factors.

Most important, perhaps, is the fact that new sonorities and sounds can be developed on tape to take the place of, or to supplement, those sounds inherent in traditional instruments. This is a reminder that the "shrill" violin once replaced the "noble" viol; the "tinny" pianoforte usurped the position of the "majestic" harpsichord; and so on and on throughout history. Such new possibilities are exciting to many Twentieth-Century composers, and although such music may be in its experimental stage at this time, the idiom is developing rapidly, and we should try to understand the logic of this development regardless of our personal inclinations and sentiments.

EXERCISES

1) Compose a short piece for unaccompanied clarinet or flute, using octave displacements. Employ a mixture of dissonant and consonant melodic intervals and follow the rules of melodic writing, as discussed in this chapter.

2) Compose a piece for violin and viola or flute and clarinet, depending upon the availability of these instruments in class. Keep the style predominantly dissonant, but use only a few large leaps and octave displacements. Watch equal high points and plot the curves of the separate lines with care.

3) Write a two-part invention for piano. Employ either a smooth or jagged style but avoid melodic and rhythmic sequences.

4) Compose a short piece for eight brass or woodwind instruments, in which two basic lines are doubled in two, three, and four voices.

5) Compose a piece for oboe (or flute), clarinet, and bassoon (or bass clarinet). Employ octave displacements in the bass line with the upper parts moving more smoothly.

6) Compose a slow movement for four woodwinds or string quartet in a pointillistic style.

7) Compose a short fast movement for four woodwinds in any style discussed in this chapter.

8) Select a short poem and write a piece for four-part mixed chorus, unaccom-

panied. Consider the chorus to be a good university choir.

9) Write a relatively dissonant song for soprano with piano accompaniment. Study the text carefully before choosing the style.

SCHEDULING SUGGESTIONS

Continue the study of scores and phonograph recordings. A minimum of one month should be spent on this chapter.

7 / the twelve-tone technique

Even if we do not plan to compose in the twelve-tone idiom, we must recognize the fact that thousands of composers, great and small, do so, and we will never understand their music throughly until we have attempted to utilize this technique in composition. Furthermore, an understanding may, and should, lead to further detailed study.

Essentially, the twelve-tone technique, developed by Arnold Schoenberg in the early 1920's, is another way of controlling non-tonal lines and textures. The technique has since been expanded from an ordered arrangement of the twelve half steps of our chromatic scale to "serial music" which, in reality, may include an additional ordering of dynamics, articulation of tones, and the duration of these tones. It is not within the province of an introductory book such as this to discuss the complex and often shadowy world of serial music. There are special books and articles on this subject which should be studied after an initial understanding of twelve-tone music is reached.

As we know, the basic difficulty in composing in a non-tonal idiom is intelligent control of melodic and harmonic forces: the danger of "wanderitis," so to speak. As we have noted in the first chapters of this book, there are ways of harnessing these forces by contrapuntal and harmonic means that are similar to those used in the early development of Western polyphony.

However, other Twentieth-Century composers sought additional means of controlling these new sounds by weaving semi-concealed threads of unity throughout their works. In a sense, such a technique may be compared with another feature of early Western music, the "isorhythm" of Fourteenth-Century motets.

In many of these motets rhythmic and melodic patterns were reiterated in various alterations (including diminution and augmentation) in the lowest line of the motet (tenor) and at times in all voices. These semi-concealed patterns instilled unity in the works without always making the listener aware of the reason. The parallel in twelve-tone music will be apparent.

Twelve-tone music is essentially contrapuntal, although harmonic formations, as we shall find, are also employed. Rules have been formulated as guides by various theorists—as in all musical ages—but certain flexibilities are inherent within the style. However, for the person being introduced to the twelve-tone technique (not "method") for the first time, rule expansions should be avoided until the basic essentials are understood. After that, scores should be studied carefully to obtain further understanding of a constantly expanding idiom that has also entered the realm of electronic music.

THE TONE-ROW The foundation upon which the twelve-tone technique is based is the tone-row which may also be referred to as the "basic set," the "twelve-tone series," or simply the "row." This tone-row, which is based on an arrangement of the twelve half steps of the chromatic scale, will be the germinating factor of our music and will produce the thread that will give unity to our writing. In its basic form, without meter and rhythm, the row is useless, but we shall see that our composition will spring from its intervallic relationships.

In essence, twelve-tone music denies traditional key relationships and chordal forms, since major and minor triads are considered to be foreign to the idiom. Thus, in using the twelve half steps of the chromatic scale to form our basic row, we should avoid the following outline.

Ex. 1

Furthermore, it is advisable to avoid using too many melodic intervals of the same or similar size, since these may lead to melodic monotony.

Ex. 2

187

When setting up a twelve-tone series, one should choose some melodic intervals which can be identified later as developmental patterns in a composition. This is, of course, basic in composing a developmental theme in any style, traditional or atonal. For example, notice in the following row the inclusion of a perfect fifth (invertible as a perfect fourth) and a minor sixth (invertible as a major third). With the various half steps and other intervals, these descending or ascending leaps may be used effectively when writing the finished work.

3 Schoenberg *Fourth String Quartet*
Copyright 1939, by G. Schirmer, Inc. Reprinted by permission.

Alban Berg uses the following row in his *Lyric Suite* for string quartet.

4 Berg *Lyric Suite*

But in his *Violin Concerto*, Berg constructed a series which could lead to the more traditional use of the triad in all of its forms—an arrangement that is frowned upon in most dodecaphonic circles.

5 Berg *Violin Concerto*
  Reprinted by permission of Universal Edition, A. G., Vienna and Associated Music Publisher Inc., New York.

Anton Webern employs the following row in his *Symphony*, Op. 21.

6 Webern *Symphony*, Op. 21
  Reprinted by permission of Universal Edition A. G., Vienna and Associated Music Publishers, Inc., New York.

The basic row or series is, therefore, carefully plotted in order to provide effective melodic and harmonic material for a composition. When it is first written, the row is normally notated as illustrated in the preceding examples: whole notes without barlines. However, when we use the tone-row in our composition, each tone may appear in any octave—an A is an A no matter in which octave it appears. Furthermore, since we are working with equal temperament, sharps and flats are used solely for the convenience of the performer and thus, G♯ and A♭ are identical.

In addition to the original row (symbolized as O), three derivative rows are obtained: Retrograde (R), Inversion (I), and Retrograde Inversion (RI). In the first movement of Schoenberg's *Fourth String Quartet,* the four series are as follows:

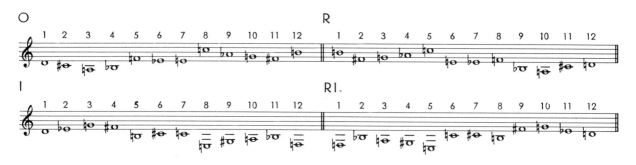

7 Schoenberg *Fourth String Quartet*
Copyright, 1939, by G. Schirmer, Inc. Reprinted by permission.

We see in Example 7 that the R series consists of O written backwards: I is an exact inversion of O; and RI is I written backwards.

MELODIC WRITING As we have noted, the four series are useless in their basic forms until we add meter, rhythm, and dynamics. In adding these elements, however, we must follow certain rules, the first of which has already been mentioned:

1) Any tone may be written in any octave.

For example, Schoenberg presents his original row (O) as follows at the beginning of the first movement.

8 Schoenberg *Fourth String Quartet* (p. 1)
Copyright, 1939, by G. Schirmer, Inc. Reprinted by permission.

However, he could have written the same passage as follows, for any note in the twelve-tone series may appear in any octave.

191

Ex. 9

2) The sequence of tones in each of the four series must be retained.

In other words, the first tone of a row must be followed by the second through the twelfth note as seen in the examples above. Therefore, no tone may be repeated out of sequence except in certain circumstances. If we re-examine Example 8, we will note that Schoenberg did repeat the third, seventh, eleventh, and twelfth tones of the original row in order to emphasize these notes, but they do not appear out of sequence.

However, a note may be repeated out of sequence *in the same* octave if it is used in trills, tremolos, or pedal figures.

10 (a) Schoenberg *Fourth String Quartet* (pp. 69–70)
Copyright, 1939, by G. Schirmer, Inc. Reprinted by permission.

10 (b) Schoenberg *Fourth String Quartet* (p. 10)
Copyright, 1939, by G. Schirmer, Inc. Reprinted by permission

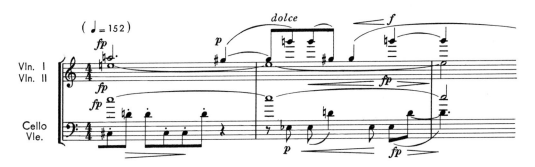

10 (c) Schoenberg *Fourth String Quartet* (p. 16)
Copyright, 1939, by G. Schirmer, Inc. Reprinted by permission.

Or a tone may be repeated out of sequence in the same octave in a tremolo-like pattern.

11 Schoenberg *Fourth String Quartet* (pp. 5-6)
Copyright, 1939, by G. Schirmer, Inc. Reprinted by permission.

There are other exceptions to this rule which need not detain us in this introductory book, but in general, a note may only be repeated out of sequence if it is an obvious part of a repetitive pattern.

3) Each of the four rows may be transposed any interval.

The original row (O) and its three derivative rows (R, I, RI) may, therefore, be transposed eleven times, allowing twelve positions for each row. We now have forty-eight serial patterns which can be used in our writing, as long as the exact sequence of intervals in each series is preserved.

For instance, Schoenberg's original row is seen in the following example transposed a diminished fifth.

12 Schoenberg *Fourth String Quartet* (p. 18)
Copyight, 1939, by G. Schirmer, Inc. Reprinted by permission.

And the inversion, transposed a perfect fourth, appears as follows.

13 Schoenberg *Fourth String Quartet* (p. 1)
Copyright, 1939, by G. Schirmer, Inc. Reprinted by permission.

We see, therefore, that the four basic series may be written in any octave, transposed any interval, and provided with any rhythm, meter, and dynamic markings as long as the sequence of tones is preserved exactly.

To these basic rules, we may add the majority of those discussed in Chapter 1: (1) avoid outlining traditional chords; (2) handle leaps from weak to strong beats with care; (3) be careful when writing more than one leap in the same direction; (4) avoid equal high and low points; (5) make the melodic line lead to some climactic goal; (6) avoid extreme melodic jaggedness during the early stages of writing in the twelve-tone style; (7) avoid using the same rhythmic pattern in consecutive or nearby measures; (8) be careful of using shifting meters—they may not be necessary or advisable; (9) avoid symmetrical phrases if possible; (10) write for available instruments, for the most part, and have exercises performed in class.

Now, let us assume that we have written the following tone-row as the basis for a composition for unaccompanied clarinet.

Ex. 14

This, in turn, generates three derivative series.

Ex. 15

And as we have seen, O, R, I, and RI may be transposed eleven times, one of these transpositions being as follows.

Ex. 16

Although we may use any or all of the forty-eight series available to us, it should be obvious that we shall not do so in a short piece, or even in long compositions. They are simply available to us in the same way that any of the keys may be used in tonal music.

At this time, let us employ only the untransposed series for our short piece for unaccompanied clarinet. We must keep in mind the sequence of tones. Otherwise, we may proceed exactly as we did in writing non-serial melodies.

Ex. 17

Note that the melody begins with untransposed O and then continues with untransposed R, RI, and I. It was not necessary for us to start with O, since there is no sequence of *series* to be preserved; only the tones within each series. Notice, also, that the twelfth tone of O (measure three) becomes the first tone of R untransposed. This interchange occurs also in measure eight in which the twelfth tone of RI is the same as the first tone of I.

The sequence of tones is undisturbed at all times, although the second note of I is repeated within the same octave in measure eight.

Except for these characteristics, which are peculiar to the twelve-tone technique, the melody is constructed in the same manner as any melodic line we have discussed in this book. One high point and one low point exist, and the melodic curve is plotted carefully. The over-all rhythmic pattern is simple and yet avoids the obvious. And if the basic set is constructed carefully, the resulting melodic lines may contain a perceptible harmonic rhythm.

Now let us use our series to compose a short melody for unaccompanied violin. This time we may employ transpositions of our basic rows in addition to the original series.

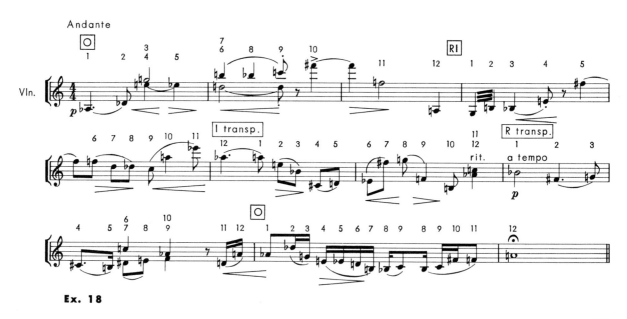

Ex. 18

In this example we used O, RI, I and R (transposed up a minor second), and untransposed O again. All tones of these series appear in sequence with several permissible exceptions. In measure four, the first two tones of RI are played out of sequence in the tremolo figure, and throughout the passage violin double stops permit the simultaneous use of adjacent tones.

The effectiveness of the melody must rest on the construction of the original tone-row, the manner in which it and its derivative series are clothed in rhythm, meter, and dynamic markings, and the way in which the melodic curves are plotted.

TWO-PART WRITING When we use the twelve-tone technique in writing for two instruments or voices, we proceed somewhat along the lines discussed in the previous chapter on highly dissonant music. By common consent, minor seconds and major sevenths are considered sharply dissonant; major seconds and minor sevenths are soft or mild dissonances; the tritone and perfect fourth are dissonant or relatively consonant depending upon the surrounding texture; the unison, thirds, the perfect fifth, sixths, and the octave are consonant.

In choosing our vertical or harmonic intervals, we mix dissonances with consonances chiefly by employing contrary and similar motion, although parallel motion may be used sparingly. However, the octave should be avoided and the unison used infrequently, when voices meet or cross in contrary motion.

When composing for two parts, one row may be divided between the voices. Schoenberg uses the untransposed O (see Example 3, page 188) as follows.

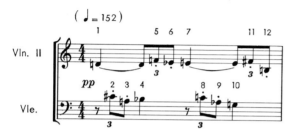

19 Schoenberg *Fourth String Quartet* (p. 3)

In this example, note that the first tone of O is sustained by the second violin while the viola plays the succeeding three notes of the row. One tone, therefore, may be sustained while other tones appear in other lines as long as the actual sequence of entering notes is not interrupted. It may also be noted that Example 19 illustrates Bach's "cartwheel" technique as it may be applied to twelve-tone music.

Again, notice how RI is divided between the first and second violins in the following excerpt.

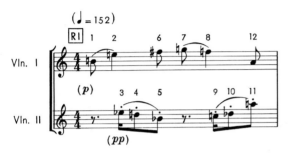

20 Schoenberg *Fourth String Quartet* (p. 22)

In the following example from the first movement of the same quartet, untransposed I is allotted to the first violin while the cello plays O transposed a perfect fifth.

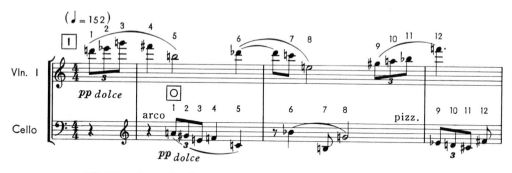

21 Schoenberg *Fourth String Quartet* (p. 8)

The four basic rows and their transpositions, therefore, may be combined in the two lines in any manner as long as the sequence of tones is maintained. For example, if we use the untransposed O and R of Examples 14 and 15, we may compose the following passage for two flutes.

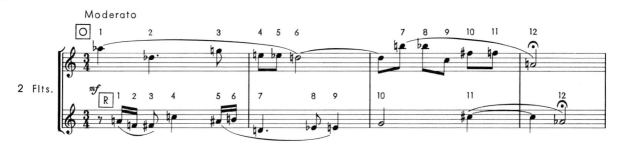

Ex. 22

The tones of these two series may also be exchanged between the two parts as follows.

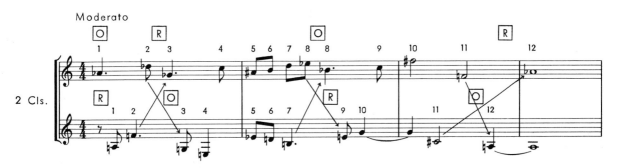

Ex. 23

Or we may use all four untransposed rows.

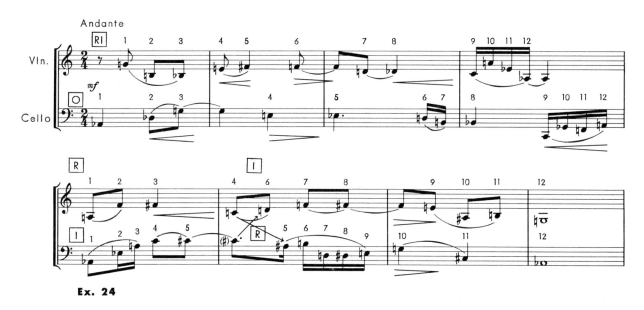

Ex. 24

It follows that untransposed and transposed series with repeated tones may be employed.

Ex. 25

MULTI-VOICE WRITING Twelve-tone composition with three or more voices presents us with many of the same problems that confronted us in preceding chapters. We must handle a more complex texture which incorporates additional intervals and more complicated rhythmic patterns. Until now, in this chapter, we have proceeded in an entirely contrapuntal manner in writing for two voices. However, we may utilize chords constructed from our series. As we shall see, this is an additional reason for writing our basic row with extreme care.

For example, an original tone-row may produce four basic triads which can be inverted and rearranged as is the case with traditional triads. The original row used by Schoenberg in the preceding excerpts from his *Fourth String Quartet* furnishes him with the following four three-note chords and inversions.

26 Schoenberg *Fourth String Quartet*
Copyright, 1939, by G. Schirmer, Inc. Reprinted by permission.

In addition, we may also use the inversion of O to produce four more chords and their inversions.

27 Schoenberg *Fourth String Quartet*
Copyright, 1939, by G. Schirmer, Inc. Reprinted by permission.

It is obvious that R and RI will produce the same chords as O and I, respectively. However, the eight different triads and their inversions may be transposed eleven times as were the basic rows.

In a like manner, we may construct four-note chords from O and I which give us six chords and their inversions to be used in all transpositions. The four-note chords based on Schoenberg's rows are as follows.

28 Schoenberg *Fourth String Quartet*
Copyright, 1939, by G. Schirmer, Inc. Reprinted by permission.

As an extension of this, we may also construct chords containing any number of tones from two through twelve which may be used as accompaniments or as block harmonies. Note, for example, how Schoenberg divides the untransposed O between all four instruments in the following passage.

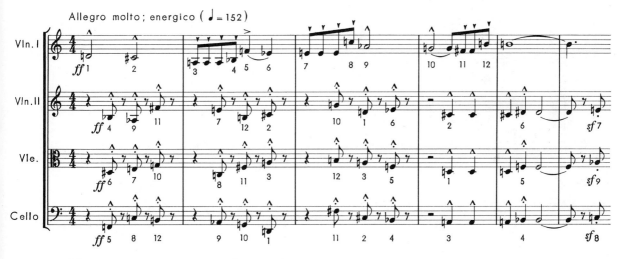

29 Schoenberg *Fourth String Quartet* (p. 1)

Copyright, 1939, by G. Schirmer, Inc. Reprinted by permission.

In the third movement of this quartet, he uses double stops to produce the following block chord based on RI transposed a minor sixth.

211

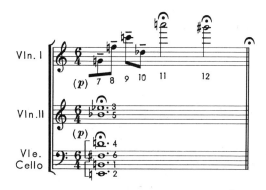

30 Schoenberg *Fourth String Quartet* (p. 65)

Copyright, 1939, by G. Schirmer, Inc. Reprinted by permission.

In order to illustrate in some detail the various contrapuntal and harmonic techniques one may use in twelve-tone composition, let us examine the first fourteen measures of the third movement from Schoenberg's *Fourth String Quartet*. Note, in particular, the following: (1) the out-of-sequence returning or neighboring tones in measures four, six, eight, and nine; (2) the substitution of the twelfth tone of transposed I for the first note of transposed O in measure twelve in the first violin part.

Notice also how he seizes upon a characteristic drop of the perfect fifth at the end of the untransposed O and imitates it in measure five of the cello part with the first two tones of the transposed RI.

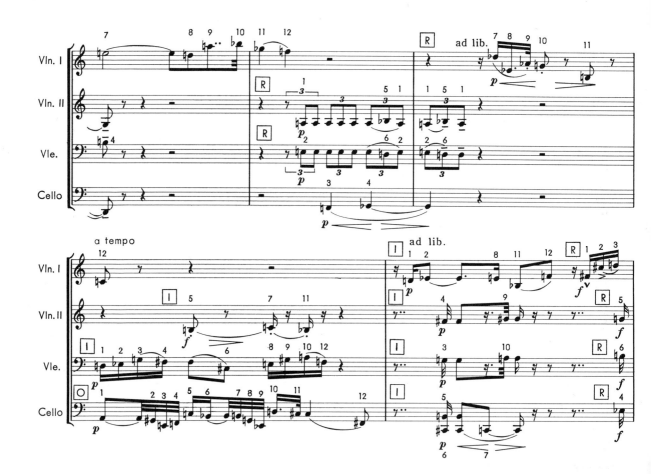

31 Schoenberg *Fourth String Quartet* (pp. 63–65)

It should be clear by now that the composer using the twelve-tone technique constructs his basic row from the standpoint of its effectiveness as developmental material, contrapuntally and harmonically.

215

As a final example, we may examine the manner in which Anton Webern's pointillistic style is expressed.

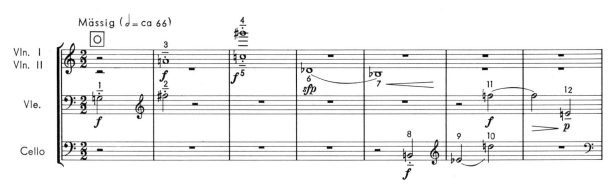

32 Webern *String Quartet,* Op. 28 (p. 1)
Reprinted by permission of Universal Edition A. G., Vienna and Associated Music Publishers, Inc., New York.

With all of this in mind, we should now work in this idiom and study scores in order to understand the true flexibilities of the technique. There are many subtleties which are incorporated into the style by Twentieth-Century composers. For us, however, such subtleties may wait.

EXERCISES

1) Construct a tone-row and three derivative rows. Use these untransposed series to compose a short piece for unaccompanied flute in a style employing octave displacements.

2) Using the series of Exercise 1 and any of their transpositions, compose a short composition for unaccompanied violin or viola. Do not employ too many large leaps.

3) Using the same series in their untransposed forms, write a two-part piece for flute and clarinet. Use any style.

4) Using the series and any of their transpositions, compose a two-part piece in any style for violin and viola or for viola and cello.

5) Construct a new tone-row and three derivative rows. Use these and any of their transpositions to compose a slow movement for piano in a flowing style.

6) Construct another tone-row and three derivative rows. Use these and any of their transpositions to compose a short work for string quartet, employing octave displacements.

7) Construct a tone-row and three derivative rows. Use these and any of their transpositions to compose a pointillistic movement for flute, oboe, clarinet, bassoon, and horn in F.

8) Construct a tone-row and three derivative rows. Use these and any of their transpositions to compose a song with piano accompaniment. Use two-, three-, and four-note chords in the accompaniment to alternate with contrapuntal sections.

SCHEDULING SUGGESTIONS

An average theory class may spend from one to two months on twelve-tone composition. Such study will give the students a thorough understanding of the idiom. Composition students obviously should study the style for a minimum of one year, depending upon a school's schedule.

8 /harmonic directions

The main purpose of this book is to provide an introduction to non-tonal Twentieth-Century styles through the manipulation of contrapuntal lines. As we have seen, these lines produce harmonic fluctuations or rhythms which can be directed much as traditional harmonic sequences are guided in tonal music. In both styles, harmonic direction is obtained by these fluctuations of consonance and dissonance and by the force of the separate lines—particularly the bass—towards their goals.

Mozart, for example, employed this interchange of consonance and dissonance in the following passage. We accept his use of harsh dissonances because of the force of the individual lines.

1. Mozart *Adagio and Fugue in C Minor, K. 546*

Johann Sebastian Bach utilized a similar technique to produce a sharply dissonant chord.

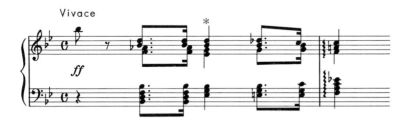

2 J. S. Bach *Well-Tempered Clavier,* Vol. I (Preludio XXI)

These two examples illustrate clearly the manner in which great composers in the past have manipulated their lines to produce sounds denied to less imaginative men. In the first seven chapters of this book, we have seen how significant Twentieth-Century composers direct their individual lines to produce even newer sonorities.

Nevertheless, not all music is contrapuntally inspired, and it may be helpful to consider some of these non-tonal chords away from the context of counterpoint. Furthermore, there are Twentieth-Century composers who retain many traditional forms, even though the latter may be clouded by the addition of dissonant tones or employed in a non-traditional manner.

TRADITIONAL TRIADS There are certain problems facing the composer who attempts to use traditional triads in Twentieth-Century composition, since they may sound banal in highly dissonant surroundings. Furthermore, forms such as the augmented triad should be handled with care, unless we are to be reminded of some of the shallow music written for films, radio, television, and dancing. The augmented triad, however, may be used in an unaccented position as follows.

Ex. 3

But a non-traditional substitute might add freshness to this passage.

221

Ex. 4

For similar reasons, the whole-tone scale is usually handled with care, because its use may conjure up artificial echos of musical impressionism. A melodic passage using sections of this scale may be veiled by an accompanying counterpoint.

Ex. 5

Diminished triads may be employed as passing chords or in other weak positions. Their use as climactic chords in Twentieth-Century music would appear to be somewhat less convincing than in the music of the last two centuries where they were regarded as the climax chord par excellence. In the following passage they do not appear foreign.

Ex. 6

Simple major and minor triads remain fresh to many ears, suggesting the indestructability of basic matter! However, as we have noted, they appear foreign in a consistently dissonant style. In more conservative Twentieth-Century music, major and minor triads may follow one another in any order and their use may disregard the rules of traditional theory. Some composers of choral music have found them particularly attractive and easy to sing, as in the following example.

Ex. 7

A similar use of triads in piano music is as follows.

8 Hindemith *Third Piano Sonata* (1st Movement)

Reprinted by permission of B. Schott's Soehne, Mainz, Schott & Co., Ltd., London and Associated Music Publishers, Inc., New York.

Simple major or minor triads may also be employed as points of relaxation preceding and following sections of tension.

9 Hindemith *Third Piano Sonata* (2nd Movement)

Reprinted by permission of B. Schott's Soehne, Mainz, Schott & Co., Ltd., London and Associated Music Publishers, Inc., New York.

OTHER TRADITIONAL CHORDS In mildly dissonant textures seventh, ninth, eleventh, and thirteenth chords may also be used with or without reference to traditional rules of theory. In highly dissonant music, however, simple forms of these chords tend to sound out of place.

A new problem faces the Twentieth-Century composer when he attempts to use more highly complex forms of these chords by guiding them according to their traditional roots. As late Nineteenth- and early Twentieth-Century composers discovered, these roots become clouded as the tones in the basic chords are altered. This clouding is seen as follows.

Root clouds ⟶

Ex. 10

In addition, if the tones in highly altered chords are rearranged, no root may be apparent to our ears, making the chords difficult to handle, at least in a tonal manner. Such chords, however, may be used with comparative ease in the contrapuntal ways discussed in the preceding chapters, that is, as combinations of intervals. This absence of a clearly definable root may be seen in the following example.

226

Ex. 11

Such chords may also be used without reference to counterpoint as splashes of color.

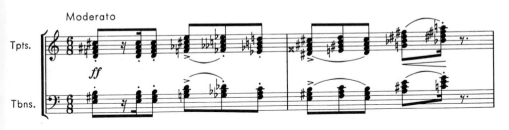

Ex. 12

It is possible to construct chords on paper which appear to be higher than thirteenths. However, such "fifteenth," "seventeenth," and even higher chords must be used with almost no tone omissions and in root positions if they are to retain perceptible roots. Roots tend to vanish with additional alterations or if the chords are inverted. For this reason, it is doubtful whether such formations should be considered as entities based on definable roots, since they too, are easily handled as intervallic combinations.

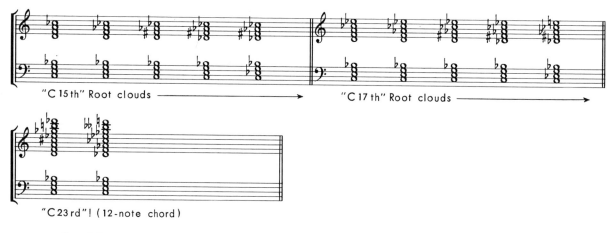

"C 15th" Root clouds ⟶   "C 17th" Root clouds ⟶

"C 23rd"! (12-note chord)

Ex. 13

Such formations may also be employed as color effects in various ways.

Ex. 14

ADDED-NOTE CHORDS Another method of using major and minor triads is to cloud them with the addition of the diatonic second or fourth.

Ex. 15

Such chords may be used with the roots proceeding traditionally.

Ex. 16

Or normal root sequences may be avoided.

Andante

Ex. 17

Such clouded triads are normally mixed with other relatively consonant forms.

Lento

2 Flts

2 Cls.

Ex. 18

These clouded triads are often used in choral writing, because they are rather easy to sing, yet produce a sort of pseudo-modern sound, which can be handled without difficulty.

231

Ex. 19

Stravinsky employs the added-note triad as follows.

20 Stravinsky *Symphony of Psalms* (3rd Movement)

We will notice that in these examples the added seconds or fourths were enclosed within the basic triad. If these tones are added in an upper octave, our ears tend to hear incomplete ninths or elevenths and the force of the chord is weakened.

Ex. 21

If an added second is placed below the root, the force of the chord remains strong, but we tend to hear an inverted ninth without a seventh.

Ex. 22

And if the added perfect fourth appears below the root, the ear may hear two simultaneous roots, which can be handled as such to guide a type of incomplete polychord.

Ex. 23

These two forms may be used as follows.

Ex. 24

If many tones foreign to the basic traditional scale are added to major and minor triads, the chords tend to lose their root feelings. Furthermore, if the added notes are not separated from the triads, the forms will sound like clusters.

Ex. 25

A cluster may comprise most or all of the chromatic steps of the scale.

Ex. 26

Small clusters may be handled easily by contrapuntal means.

235

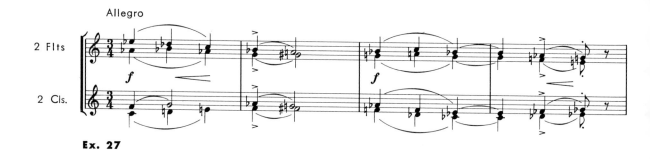

Ex. 27

Small and large clusters may be used more frequently for percussive purposes.

Ex. 28

Clusters may even be employed in choral writing.

29 Berg Wozzeck (Act II, Scene 4)

Reprinted by permission of Universal Edition A. G., Vienna and Associated Music Publishers Inc., New York.

Clusters of any size may also be employed as melodic doubling in a contrapuntal style.

Ex. 30

Another form of clouded triads contains simultaneous major and minor thirds, normally separated by one or more octaves.

Ex. 31

William Schuman employs this style as follows.

32 Schuman *String Quartet No. 4*

In general, triads with various added tones are mixed together with other forms to avoid monotony. When they are employed, the style is usually quite consonant in terms of the Twentieth Century.

Ex. 33

POLYTONALITY AND POLYCHORDS Strictly speaking, polytonality is the use of two or more traditional keys simultaneously. The resulting polychords may be employed as isolated vertical formations in any compositional style, traditional or non-traditional. We have already noted that a triad with an added fourth placed below the root at an interval of the perfect fifth tends to suggest the presence of two separate roots. (See page 234)

As we know, complete ninth, eleventh, and thirteenth chords—altered and unaltered—consist of separate triads, major, minor, augmented, and diminished.

Ex. 34

Thus, it follows that the separate but related components of such chords may be used as follows.

Moderato

String
Orch.

Ex. 35

A similar technique was employed by various composers during the early Twentieth Century, and in fact, Beethoven suggested the practice in the following excerpt.

Allegro

36 Beethoven *Sonata in E♭ for Piano, Op.* 81a

Example 35 illustrates a type of melodic doubling with traditional triads. These triads, however, must be kept separated for purposes of polytonal clarity, since if the chords are placed

241

close together, we tend to hear but one root. Furthermore, if the notes of the various chords are intermixed, the polyharmonic effect is clouded or lost.

(Clear)   (Close)   (Clouded)

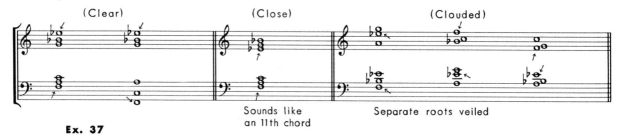

Sounds like   Separate roots veiled
an 11th chord

Ex. 37

Polychords may be spaced widely to produce a richer texture.

Moderato

String
Orch.

Ex. 38

242

And they may be used in the following manner.

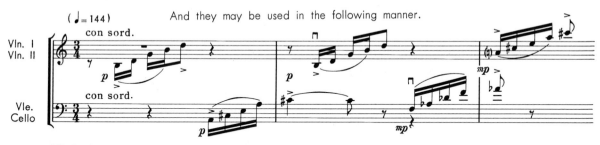

39 Copland *Sextet for String Quartet, Clarinet, and Piano* **(p.23)**
Copyright 1948 by Boosey & Hawkes Inc. Reprinted by permission.

Or they may be used as in this well-known passage from Stravinsky's *Petrouchka.*

40 Stravinsky *Petrouchka* **(p. 61)**
Copyright by Edition Russe de Musique. All rights assigned to Boosey & Hawkes Inc. Revised Edition Copyright 1947 by Boosey & Hawkes Inc. Reprinted by permission.

Two major triads with different roots normally produce a brighter sound than that achieved through the use of two minor triads. When major and minor triads with different roots are employed simultaneously, it is customary to use the major triad as the lower unit because of the resulting brightness.

Ex. 41

More than two polyharmonic units may be employed if they are separated for clarity's sake.

Ex. 42

However, the fact that the separate roots within a polychord may not be heard unless there is a separation between the units makes such chords difficult to handle. Even if clarity is maintained, the experienced ear may hear polychords as unaltered or altered traditional chords with one root. Stravinsky's famous bitonal motive in *Petrouchka* (Example 40) may impress us no longer as a combination of C and F♯ major. If a C triad is placed below an F♯ triad, we may hear an augmented eleventh chord on C. If the positions of the two triads are reversed, we may then hear an altered eleventh on F♯ sharp.

Ex. 43

For all of these reasons, this technique should be handled with care. There is, however, another possibility which may be examined: the employment of a sequence of traditional chords to accompany a melodic line comprised largely of tones foreign to these chords.

Ex. 44

As we see in Example 45, any tone may belong to an altered thirteenth chord and thus related to basic triads upon which the thirteenth chord is built. However, we should be careful that this style does not become contrived.

Ex. 45

OTHER CHORDAL FORMS Until now, this chapter has dealt with chords constructed basically on thirds; that is, founded on tertian harmony or counterpoint. When such chords became unwieldy or nebulous, owing to extended alterations applied to them in the late Nineteenth and early Twentieth Centuries—in other words, when the traditional system of tonality seemed to have been extended to its limits—certain composers attempted to erect alternate systems in which chords may be built on intervals other than thirds.

In the preceding seven chapters of this book we have actually constructed many of these chords by contrapuntal methods, but without constructing specific harmonic systems. As a matter of fact, some composers would insist that the building of such systems might lead to further harmonic impasses. Rules of voice-leading may be established to enable composers to handle such chords, but unless one mixes chords from several of all of these systems, the results may be monotonous. Furthermore, such formations may be handled with ease by the contrapuntal-harmonic methods already discussed.

However, we should be acquainted with these forms as they may be used by some Twentieth-Century composers. Perhaps the one that has been used most frequently is the chord comprising two or more perfect fourths. As the form lacks a clearly defined root (as with any chord constructed of equal intervals), it tends to have the neutral function of a diminished or augmented triad and can move in any direction.

Ex. 46

Fourth chords have been employed often as fanfares.

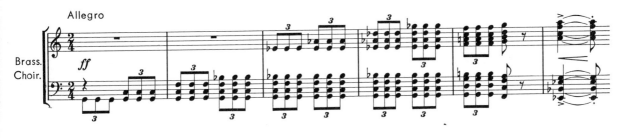

Brass.
Choir.

Ex. 47

If a chord based on perfect fourths is inverted, or if its basic order of tones is disturbed, its quality changes. The three-note form may sound like an incomplete triad (root and fifth) with an added second or fourth; the multi-note form loses its quartal characteristics and may sound like added-note or altered traditional chords.

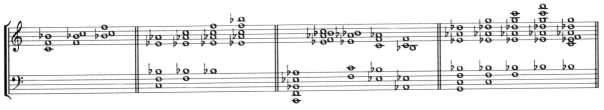

Ex. 48

Such inverted or changed forms, however, may be handled easily in a contrapuntal or harmonic manner without reference to labels.

Ex. 49

It is quite possible to erect fourth chords consisting of augmented and perfect intervals.

Ex. 50

A chord may be constructed of perfect fifths, but unless it is used in its basic form, it also loses its characteristic sound.

Ex. 51

Chords built on major or minor sevenths are sometimes used as color punctuations.

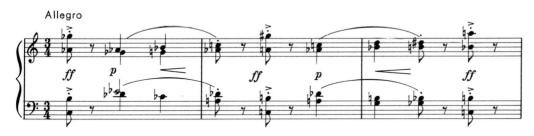

Ex. 52

However, if we erect a three-note chord on major and minor sevenths, the former should be placed below. Otherwise we tend to hear an incomplete thirteenth chord with a clearly delineated root.

Ex. 53

New systems may, therefore, be formulated on the grounds that chords may be constructed of other intervals than the third. However, because all of these forms are handled so easily without designating them as fourth chords, fifth chords, and so forth, the value of such chordal systems may be doubted, and, as we have seen, the inversion of many of these chords so destroy their basic characteristics that we may not even be certain at all times what type of chord we are really handling. A final example involves the three-note chord built on seconds.

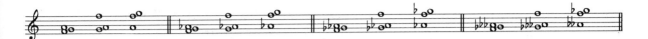

Ex. 54

If is quite possible to use these forms in the following manner.

Ex. 55

However, as one can see by performing Example 55, there is often nothing to distinguish the sounds of some of these chords from incomplete (but easily identified) traditional forms or inversions of chords constructed on other intervals. And it makes no difference whether we hear them in or out of context. The following illustration from Example 55 indicates this problem.

253

Added-Note Triad   Ninth Chord   Thirteenth Chord   Chord of Sevenths

Ex. 56

COMPOSITIONAL SUGGESTIONS In order to examine further some of the forms discussed in this chapter, let us assume that we have written the following melodic excerpt for the sopranos of a good, but far from professional, chorus.

Ex. 57

Here is a simple line which avoids outlining traditional chords directly, but may be harmonized in almost any manner. If we wish to retain some traditional harmonies, we may compose the other voices as follows.

254

Ex. 58

If we wish to retain the same harmonic idiom and yet add contrapuntal movement to the separate parts, the passage could be written in the following manner.

Ex. 59

Examine both examples and note the presence of chords that have been discussed in this chapter, but that need not be guided according to rules other than those outlined in the first chapters of this book.

This melodic excerpt may also be harmonized with a mixture of mild dissonances and consonances.

Ex. 60

The line may be harmonized also in a more dissonant manner which ignores basic traditional chords.

Ex. 61

The following example illustrates the use of veiled traditional forms with less regard for contrapuntal movement or voice-leading.

Ex. 62

Again, the dissonance may be increased.

1 Ob.
2 Cls.
Eng. Hn.

2 Bsns.

Moderato

Ex. 63

The main thing to do is to write and to *listen*. Even if we choose a more dissonant style, we should understand those compositions that employ more consonant materials.

EXERCISES

1) Compose a short work for mixed chorus using some triads with added major seconds and perfect fourths. Employ traditional and non-traditional root sequences and use the added tones in any singable octave.

2) Write a short piece for flute, clarinet, and bassoon using chords built on seconds and perfect fourths, using any inversions of these forms.

3) Compose a short piece for four horns in F employing clusters and chords built on major seconds and perfect fourths.

258

4) Compose a slow movement for string quartet using a mixture of triads with simultaneous major and minor thirds, added-note triads, clusters, and chords built on seconds and perfect fourths.

5) Write a short piece for eight brass instruments (four trumpets and four trombones; or two trumpets, two horns in F, three trombones, and one tuba), which employs polychords and other forms discussed in this chapter.

6) Compose a song with piano accompaniment using any chords discussed in this chapter.

SCHEDULING SUGGESTIONS

This chapter may be considered as a sort of "appendix" to a course in contemporary practices. Serious work in the preceding chapters should allow the students to work with these chordal forms with comparative ease. Although many teachers may doubt the wisdom of returning to tonal forms even to obtain an understanding of their use by many composers, they should not be studied *before* the non-tonal procedures discussed in the first seven chapters if we are to gain a true understanding of atonal idioms.

9 / *postlude*

This book is concerned chiefly with counterpoint, in recognition of the historical fact that harmony has been largely a product of contrapuntal lines. This was true of modally based music during the Middle Ages and the Renaissance, of the tonally based music of the Baroque, the Eighteenth and Nineteenth centuries, and of much of the non-tonal music of the present century.

This is not to say that counterpoint is the means to all ends, or that all music is contrapuntal. However, the composer who learns to handle and to identify non-traditional chords through contrapuntal practice will have no difficulty using these same chords in a purely harmonic or vertical manner. This was as true of Gesualdo as it was of Schoenberg or Bartók.

The conductor, performer, or intellectually curious listener will gain an understanding of non-tonal composition in the same manner: by writing in the general styles used by Twentieth-Century composers, great and small.

The person who has studied this book seriously should now realize that he will never know *enough* about music theory—contrapuntal or harmonic, contemporary or traditional. But he should now be able to carry on by himself and to further his knowledge. He should realize that all musical innovations throughout the course of Western history have contributed something to the evolution of the art and that all new styles are an extension in some way or another of those that preceded them.

Tonal and atonal explorations in the realm of sonority—controlled sound—have led to newer explorations in laboratories or electronic studios. This pioneering in the areas of *musique concrète* and electronic music is also an extension of traditional and non-traditional explorations. And microtones lie at the top of the overtone series and do not defy understanding even though they may continue for some time to defy the capabilities of the Western ear.

It is the artistic and intellectual duty of people who call themselves musicians to study the experiments and the mature conclusions of those pioneers who have existed in every historical age. Such a study not only helps to create the great composers of each period, but also endows the great mass of us who possess lesser gifts with a certain humility—that quality which encourages us to confront all things, new and old, with an objective and ever-curious mind.

Further references

Basart, Ann Phillips, *Serial Music*. A Classified Bibliography of Writings on Twelve-Tone and Electronic Music. Berkeley, Calif.: University of California Press, 1961.

Cooper, Grosvenor W., *The Rhythmic Structure of Music*. Chicago: University of Chicago Press, 1960.

Dallin, Leon, *Techniques of Twentieth-Century Composition*. Dubuque, Iowa: William C. Brown Company, 1957.

Forte, Allen, *Contemporary Tone-Structures*. New York: Columbia University Press, 1955.

Graves, William L., *Twentieth-Century Fugue*. Washington, D. C.: Catholic University of America, 1962.

Hanson, Howard, *The Harmonic Materials of Modern Music*. New York: Appleton-Century-Crofts, Inc., 1960.

Hiller, Lejaren and Leonard Isaacson, *Experimental Music*. New York: McGraw-Hill Inc., 1959.

Hindemith, Paul, *The Craft of Musical Composition*. New York: Associated Music Publishers, 1945.

Kanitz, Ernest, *A Counterpoint Workbook*. Ann Arbor, Mich.: Edwards Brothers, 1947.

Krenek, Ernst, *Studies in Counterpoint*. New York: G. Schirmer, Inc., 1940.

Leibowitz, René, *Schoenberg and His School*. New York: Philosophical Library, Inc., 1949.

Messiaen, Oliver, *The Technique of My Musical Language*. Paris, France: A. Leduc, 1956.

Perle, George, *Serial Composition and Atonality*. Berkeley, Calif.: University of California Press, 1962.

Persichetti, Vincent, *Twentieth-Century Harmony*. New York: W. W. Norton & Company, Inc., 1961

Reti, Rudolph R., *Tonality in Modern Music*. New York: Collier Books, 1962.

Rochberg, George, *The Hexachord and its Relation to the 12-Tone Row*. Bryn Mawr, Penna.: Theodore Presser, 1955.

Rufer, Josef, *Composition with Twelve Notes Related to One Another*. London: Rockliff, 1954.

Schoenberg, Arnold, *Style and Idea*. New York: Philosophical Library, Inc., 1950.

Searle, Humphrey, *Twentieth-Century Counterpoint*. New York: John de Graff, Inc., 1954.

262

Spinner, Leopold, *A Short Introduction to the Technique of Twelve-Tone Composition*. London: Boosey & Hawkes Ltd., 1960.

Stevens, Halsey, *The Life and Music of Bela Bartok*. New York: Oxford University Press, 1953.

The following journals may be consulted for further references:

American Composers Alliance Bulletin, New York.

Journal of Music Theory, Yale School of Music, New Haven, Connecticut.

Music & Letters, Oxford University Press, London.

Musical Quarterly, G. Schirmer, New York.

Perspectives of New Music, Princeton University Press, Princeton, New Jersey.

Reihe, Die, Theodore Presser, Bryn Mawr, Pennsylvania.

Tempo, Boosey & Hawkes, London.

INDEX

A

Accidentals, notation of, 7
Added-note chords, 229 ff., 249, 254
Altered chords, 226-227, 240, 245, 247, 249
Aristophanes, 23
Augmentation, 153, 186

B

Bach, J. S., 5, 148
   "Cartwheel" technique, 61 ff., 70, 103, 202
   Two-part inventions, 61
   Well-tempered Clavier, 220
Barline displacement, 31-32, 39
Bartok, Bela, 6, 260
   Concerto for Violin, 12, 18
   Miraculous Mandarin, 6
   String Quartet No. 1, 26, 40-41
   String Quartet No. 5, 130, 139
   String Quartet No. 6, 130-131
Beethoven, Ludwig van, 1, 2, 5, 46, 182
   Great Fugue, 2-3, 4, 163

Sonata for Piano, Op. 13, 24-25
Sonata for Piano, Op. 81a, 4, 241
Sonata for Piano, Op. 106, 55
Sonata for Piano, Op. 111, 47
String Quartet, Op. 59, No. 1, 179
Berg, Alban
   Chamber Concerto, 22, 26
   Lyric Suite, 167, 188
   Violin Concerto, 189
   Wozzeck, 171-172, 237
Berlioz, Hector, 1, 182

C

Canonic writing, 138-139
Carter, Elliott
   String Quartet (1951), 62, 73-74, 162-163, 174
"Cartwheel Technique" (See Bach)
Chords
   by fifths, 251
   by fourths, 248 ff.
   by seconds, 252 ff.

265